Mute Vol 2 #15

GREY GOO

Published by Mute Publishing Ltd., 2010

MUTE VOL 2 #15
SPRING ISSUE – APRIL '10

EDITOR

Josephine Berry Slater <josie@metamute.org>

PUBLISHERS

Pauline van Mourik Broekman
<pauline@metamute.org> and
Simon Worthington <simon@metamute.org>

ISSUE DESIGN

Laura Oldenbourg <laura@metamute.org>

ADVERTISING & MARKETING

Lois Olmstead <lois@metamute.org>
T: +44 (0)20 3287 9005

WEBSITE

Metamute.org is powered by Drupal and CiviCRM FLOSS Software, with additional software services by our very own OpenMute http://openmute.org

TECH SUPPORT

Web infrastructure: Darron Broad
<darron@kewl.org>

PROJECT ASSISTANT CO-ORDINATOR

Caroline Heron <caroline@metamute.org>

INTERNS

Scott Lenney and Andrea Tocchini

OFFICE

Mute, 46 Lexington Street, London, W1F 0LP
T: +44 (0)20 3287 9005
email: <mute@metamute.org>

SUBSCRIPTIONS

Howard Slater
T: +44 (0)20 3287 9005
email: <howard@metamute.org>
web: http://www.metamute.org/subs

DISTRIBUTION UK

Central Books, 99 Wallis Road, London, E4 5LN
T: +44 (0)20 8986 4854
F: +44 (0)20 8533 5821
email: <mark@centralbooks.com>

DISTRIBUTION NORTH AMERICA

Please contact: Lois Olmstead
<lois@metamute.org> T: +44 (0)20 3287 9005

CONTRIBUTING

Mute welcomes contributions of all kinds. Email <mute@metamute.org> with your ideas
You can also publish on Mute's website [http://www.metamute.org]. Post news, texts, events and comments, or upload media.
The views expressed in Mute and Metamute are not necessarily those of the publishers or service providers. Mute is published in the UK by Mute Publishing Ltd. and printed by OpenMute [http://openmute.org] print on demand (POD) book services in the USA and UK.

COVER

Martin Howse <m@10.10.co.uk>

SPECIAL THANKS

To Caroline Heron for superhuman lifting and logistical prowess, and to Max for wisecracking all the way to Peterborough.

ISSN 1356-7748 - 215
ISBN 978-1-906496-45-6

Contents

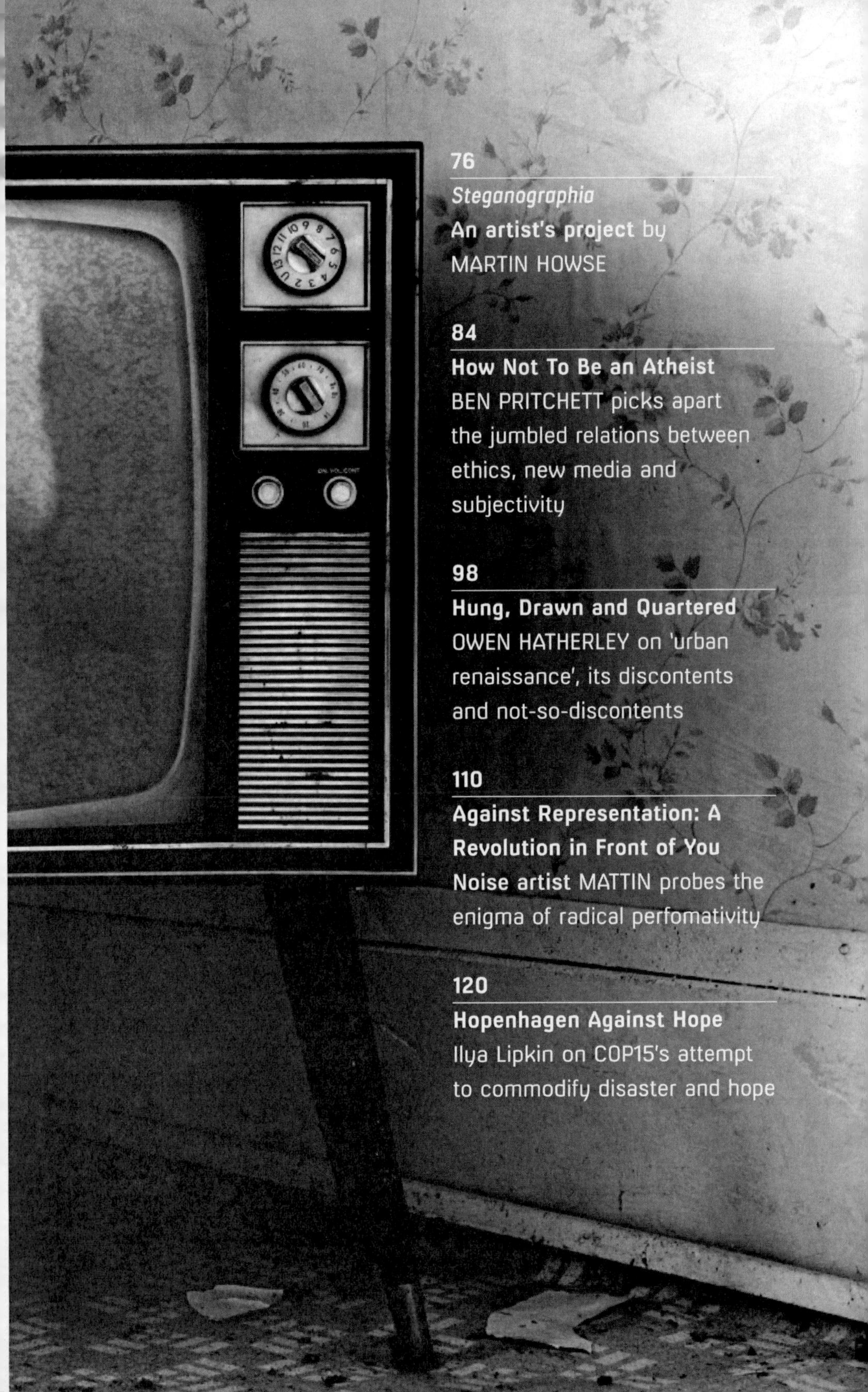

EDITORIAL

Grey goo is a hypothetical end-of-the-world scenario involving molecular nanotechnology in which out-of-control self-replicating robots consume all matter on Earth while building more of themselves, [...] a scenario known as ecophagy ('eating the environment'). [...] Self-replicating machines of the macroscopic variety were originally described by mathematician John von Neumann, and are sometimes referred to as von Neumann machines. The term grey goo was coined by nanotechnology pioneer Eric Drexler in his 1986 book Engines of Creation.

– Wikipedia.org

The joy of this spectacularly dystopian meme is not only that it provides a sci-fi analogue for the carnage reaped by capital accumulation but also that it conceives of its residue – a world not definitively destroyed, but degenerated into a mass of undifferentiated, yet still active goo. The goo's combination of inhuman self-replication and destruction is a Marxist's wet dream, but also an image of how the pop imaginary conceives of The End. Not as a break ushering in the transvaluation of all values, but as an infinite extension of more of the same old shit. In this issue of *Mute* we are thinking through the prospect of The End in all its divergence: its lure for revolutionary dreams, Hollywood scaremongering, the extension of markets into the atmosphere, the defensive cleavage to old models of security such as the family, the general expansion of cynicism.

As Evan Calder Williams discusses in his article [p.32] seeking to explain the recent explosion in Hollywood catastrophe movies, crisis, catastrophe and apocalypse are all highly specific terms. While apocalypse offers a moment of insight and reordering, crisis offers the insight without the reordering, and catastrophe is simply a disastrous breakdown without either possibility. Hollywood, which favours the latter, is a grey goo spewing macro-bot, and will doubtless soon be rendering this specific end-of-world scenario in one of its dreamworks.

Beyond the saturated pixels of spectacular ecophagy, there is a greyness that descends when encountering the institutional logic powering culture as it teeters on the brink of the double dip's second dip. JJ Charlesworth in his piece on London's Institute for Contemporary Arts [p.20] shows how omnivorous neoliberal logic has claimed casualties in terms of the institution's perilous dependence on sponsorship, its management style and the culture it values. As its director Ekow Eshun is quoted as saying in a vision document, 'All that matters is now.' A conviction which quickly breaks down into the formula: more celebrities equals more sponsorship cash.

The oppressiveness of this tautological manoeuvre whereby what is already present is endlessly represented because it is already present, finds its parallels in management cultures. Pop eats itself at one end of the scale, while at the other, circuits of time-wasting, self-affirming procedures proliferate (sociophagy perhaps?). Mark Fisher gave a stark example of this in a presentation on the NuBureaucracy this February at Goldsmiths University: the requirement for students to fill out feedback forms at universities to maintain their department's funding levels results in lecturers pressurising them to give positive responses so as not to jeopardise funding, so they, in turn, receive a good degree from a credible university which will actually count for something in the work place. This circuit he described as 'consensual cynicism'.

The excerpt from Matthew Fuller's forthcoming novel *Elephant & Castle* [p.62] deals with the grey goo's proliferation through techno-managerial processes, but without Fisher's restorative faith in the possibility of a socially useful bureaucracy. Fuller's story describes, with polymorphous perversity, the way a system makes use of itself and its operatives at every imaginable scale to self-replicate for an entirely obscure purpose. 'This', he writes, describing a management chief's vision of the system's life-sucking upgrade, 'is a move of incorporation which thrills participants in its capacity for swallowing.' This sounds like capitalism's standard response to resistance – if it can't be stopped it can always be assimilated.

In his article on the Copenhagen summit on climate change, Ilya Lipkin describes the self-defeating desire to turn environmental chaos into yet another basis of scarcity and value; a refusal to see its challenge as the life-threatening limit to capitalism's operative logic that it actually is. Recognising a limit to production's ceaseless expansion would be to acknowledge that not everything can or should be swallowed.

Behind the reified appearance of normality – in which business as usual seems unstoppable, climate change seems like manageable collateral damage etc. – anti-capitalist theorists are always looking for the real 'tendency', writes Benjamin Noys [p.44]. This is where the surface appearance of normality and stasis melts, at a deeper level, into a 'truer' picture of the flows of historical movement. In the minds of some theorists, however, obscured 'tendency' becomes more real than actuality, and a disconnect occurs, taking political philosophy onto the level of fantastical imaginings, many of which are apocalyptic! Noys wants to remind us that what is hidden is sometimes very different from the picture of accelerated capitalist expansion (and hence rupture) we are often led to believe in. Instead of falling for the prospect of an apocalyptic crash-and-burn scenario and accompanying new dawn, we need to look at something closer to a grey goo scenario in which a deeper homoeostasis is achieved by a system indefinitely dragging out its endgame as a survival strategy. Sober insight is never easy (much less sobriety!), but the benumbing solace of Hollywood style catastrophe, and even pseudo-apocalypse is thankfully starting to wear thin.

Josephine Berry Slater <josie@metamute.org> is Editor of *Mute* and reformed pram pusher

Rethinking Curating

Art after New Media

Beryl Graham and Sarah Cook

"The processes of displaying, collecting, and interpreting new media artworks offer considerable challenges to individuals and institutions across the contemporary art world. New media projects and exhibitions are innately complex. And whatever their complexity, they frequently involve much higher levels of public participation and interactivity. In this context, Beryl Graham and Sarah Cook's Rethinking Curating *provides an intelligent, well-informed, and creative analysis which will be immensely valuable for the better understanding of this fast-changing field."*
— **Sandy Nairne**, Director, National Portrait Gallery, London

£25.95 • cloth • 369 pp. (68 illus.) • 978-0-262-01388-8

Sonic Warfare

Sound, Affect, and the Ecology of Fear

Steve Goodman

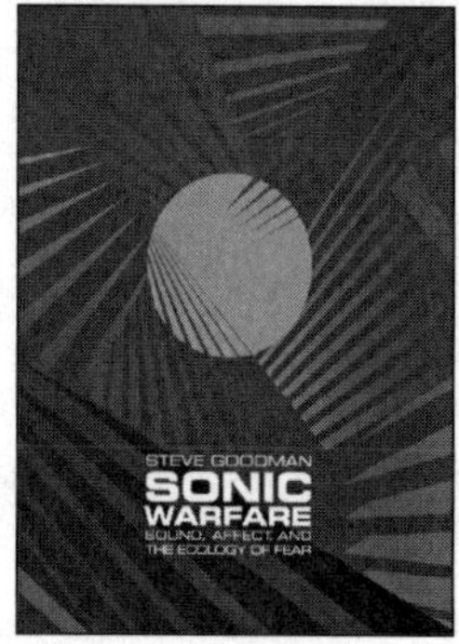

In *Sonic Warfare*, Steve Goodman explores the different uses of acoustic force and how they affect populations. Sound can be deployed to produce discomfort, express a threat, or create an ambience of fear or dread. Sonic weapons of this sort include the "psychoacoustic correction" aimed at the Branch Davidians in Waco by the FBI, sonic booms (or "sound bombs") over the Gaza Strip, and high-frequency rat repellents used against teenagers in malls. At the same time, artists and musicians generate intense frequencies in the search for new aesthetic experiences and new ways of mobilising bodies in rhythm.

£25.95 • cloth • 290 pp. • 978-0-262-01347-5

Entangled

Technology and the Transformation of Performance

Chris Salter

In *Entangled*, Chris Salter shows that technologies, from the mechanical to the computational, have been entangled with performance across a wide range of disciplines. Salter examines the rich and extensive history of performance experimentation in theatre, music, dance, the visual and media arts, architecture, and other fields. He explores the political, social, and economic context for the adoption of technological practices in art, and shows that these practices have a set of common histories despite their disciplinary borders.

£29.95 • cloth • 473 pp. (78 illus.) • 978-0-262-19588-1

The Warcraft Civilization

Social Science in a Virtual World

William Sims Bainbridge

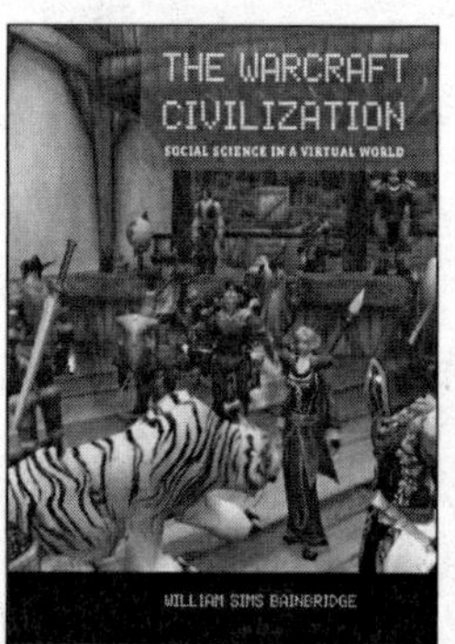

World of Warcraft is an immersive virtual world in which characters must cope in a dangerous environment, assume identities, struggle to understand and communicate, learn to use technology, and compete for dwindling resources. Beyond the fantasy and science fiction details it's not entirely unlike today's world. Sociologist William Bainbridge explores the game as a virtual prototype of the real human future, and the insights it gives as a bridge to the past and future.

£20.95 • cloth • 248 pp. (32 illus.) • 978-0-262-01370-3

VISIONS, DIVISIONS AND REVISIONS: POLITICAL FILM AND FILM THEORY IN THE 1970S AND 80S

'Visions, Divisions and Revisions' revisits the idea of 'film as a political practice', as it was practiced and theorised in the 1970s and 80s in the UK. Over the course of six events we will look at some of the key debates that enlivened these years: issues around authorship; the role of the audience; the relation of theory to practice; the use of psychoanalysis in film; and different ideas of collectivity.

Monday 8 March, 7pm
NIGHTCLEANERS (1975)
BY BERWICK STREET FILM COLLECTIVE
Screening and discussion with
Humphry Trevelyan.

Tuesday 9 March, 7pm
EDINBURGH INTERNATIONAL FILM FESTIVAL
IN THE 1970S: A PANEL DISCUSSION
With Esther Leslie (chair), Paul Willemen,
Colin MacCabe, Margaret Dickinson,
Noreen MacDowell and Felicity Sparrow.

Wednesday 17 March, 7pm
DEUX FOIS (1969) BY JACKIE RAYNAL
Screening and discussion with
Marina Vishmidt and Nina Power.

Wednesday 21 April, 7pm
LONDON WOMEN'S FILM GROUP
Screening of *Women of the Rhondda* (1972) produced by Esther Ronay, Mary Kelly, Mary Capps, Humphry Trevelyan, and *The Amazing Equal Pay Show* (1974) by the London Women's Film Group. Discussion with Julia Knight and Felicity Sparrow.

Saturday 24 April, 3pm
CINEMA ACTION
Screenings of *So That You Can Live* (1982) by Cinema Action and *Year of the Beaver* (1985) by Steve Sprung/Poster Collective. Discussion with Alex Sainsbury and Steve Sprung.

Wednesday 28 April, 7pm
DIFFERENT PERSPECTIVES
A talk with Peter Osborne and guest.

This programme takes place during the exhibition 'A History of Irritated Material' at Raven Row, 25 February to 2 May 2010.

Events are free but booking is essential as space is limited. Please email info@ravenrow.org to reserve a place.

Programme organised by Petra Bauer and Dan Kidner

Petra Bauer's first solo exhibition in the UK, 'You, Me, Us, Them', will take place at Focal Point Gallery between 27 March and 8 May 2010. Focal Point Gallery, Southend Central Library, Victoria Avenue, Southend-on-Sea SS2 6EX, T 01702 534108 www.focalpoint.org.uk

Raven Row
56 Artillery Lane
London E1 7LS
T +44 (0)20 7377 4300
info@ravenrow.org
www.ravenrow.org

BB4

Bucharest Biennale 4

Bucharest International Biennial for Contemporary Art

May 21–July 25 2010

Bienala Internațională de Artă Contemporană București

21 Mai–25 Iulie 2010

Handlung. On Producing Possibilities

Curated by Felix Vogel

Co-directed by Răzvan Ion & Eugen Rădescu

Generated by Pavilion - journal for politics and culture

www.bucharestbiennale.org I www.pavilionmagazine.org

PROUD TO BE FLESH

A MUTE MAGAZINE ANTHOLOGY OF CULTURAL POLITICS AFTER THE NET

Edited by Josephine Berry Slater and Pauline van Mourik Broekman

MUTE
Culture and Politics after the Net

A

ARTS COUNCIL
ENGLAND

MUTE
MAGA
ZINE
INTRODUCTION BY ADRIAN SHAUGHNESSY
GRAPH
IC DESIGN
eightbooks

mute
>alt.zombie.golf.the.earth

mute
OUT OF CONTROL?
mute
mute
MONGREL

Ceci n'est pas
(We've crossed oceans of time to find you...)
un magazine

MUTE
THE ART ISSUE
MUTE
INFO-WAR

CRISIS AT THE ICA: EKOW ESHUN'S EXPERIMENT IN DEINSTITUTION-ALISATION

Amidst a general acceptance of the cash crisis afflicting the ICA as an accident of the recession, and a rush into 'hair-shirt' institutional self-critique as a means to deflect real scrutiny, JJ Charlesworth uncovers a catalogue of avoidable mistakes and the free-market, lifestyle thinking behind them

In the last few weeks press reports have begun to appear regarding the growing financial crisis besetting London's Institute of Contemporary Arts. On the 22 January, the *Guardian* reported that 'Staff members have been told that a financial deficit currently at around £600,000 might rise to £1.2m and if radical steps are not taken the ICA could be closed by May.' A week later, the *Times* quoted an ICA spokeswoman who confirmed as a 'fair estimate' that 'a third of its full-time staff of "around 60" would be in line for redundancy.'

Ekow Eshun, the ICA's artistic director since 2005, told the *Guardian* that the ICA's financial problems emerged as a result of a 'perfect storm of events that all came together'. Income from fundraising, from trading income and from the ICA's film distribution arm, have 'also suffered because of the recession.'

Image: Billy Childish at the Figures of Speech gala, 2009

So far, the mainstream press has accepted this rather glib account of inevitable woe caused by the recession. In the fatalistic and passive terms that currently dominate any discussion about the recession, there is apparently nothing that anyone can do about the ICA's financial troubles; the recession is seen as a force of nature, and everyone is quick to accept Eshun's catchy characterisation of the ICA's crisis as a 'perfect storm'. So instead of asking how exactly the ICA has got into such a mess, mainstream press coverage has typically discovered another opportunity to beat-up on the ICA, and to carp about whether the ICA should be left to fail; 'should we let the ICA die?' was the *Times*' dismissive headline.

That so little interest has been paid to the precise circumstances of the ICA's troubles is disturbing. Merely accepting that 'the recession is to blame' leaves bigger questions unanswered both about the ICA's artistic and financial governance over the last five years, but also of broader issues of state funding policy towards private sector involvement in the financing of arts organisations, while making no one accountable for the roots of these failures. A closer look at the recent history of the ICA suggests a number of serious issues that have consequences not only for the future of the organisation itself, but also for the broader sector of state funded arts organisations.

In October 2009, Arts Council England awarded the ICA £1.2 million over two years from its Sustain emergency budget, ear-marked for arts organisations suffering from the effects of the recession. This is the second largest of the grants made from the fund (only the Yorkshire Sculpture Park has been granted more). As part of this emergency package a consultant, ex-curator David Thorp, had been hired to conduct an organisational review of the ICA's activities and structures. On 10 December 2009 staff were called to a meeting with Eshun and members of the ICA's governing council, including chairman Alan Yentob. In minutes of that meeting seen by the *Guardian* and by *Mute*, staff were told about the need to slash the £2.5 million salary budget by £1m, and drastically reduce the ICA's programming, particularly the cinema's programme. An organisational restructure outline also seen by *Mute* proposes closing the ICA to the public two days a week. According to Eshun, the proposed new programme would operate only in the lower exhibitions gallery.

It may have been a 'perfect storm', but someone was sailing the ship towards it

In what was clearly a heated and bad tempered debate, Eshun and Yentob continually insisted that the cash crisis was down to 'shortcomings' in the Development department, the bookshop and ICA films. Clearly defensive, Eshun argued that it was not always easy to make correct estimates, but that while this could be seen to be a result of decisions made by Eshun and Guy Perricone (Eshun's managing director, an ex-banker who finally resigned in October 2009, having been appointed shortly after Eshun in August 2005) there were 'structural problems' that needed addressing. Remarkably, Eshun concluded that he was the best person to take the ICA 'into the future'.

But the assertion that the ICA's financial difficulties are uniquely a product of the current recession does not seem to be supported by a review of the organisation's published finances in the years *prior* to the recession, and during the boom years of Eshun's tenure, since his appointment in May 2005. The ICA's accounts are publicly available through the Charities Commission. What they reveal is an organisation which, while faring relatively well from its programming income, became dangerously dependent on a high-risk strategy of developing what turned out to be volatile and unpredictable income from sponsorship deals. A later decision to remove entrance fees was to prove similarly damaging.

Under Eshun, the ICA went from an income of just over £3.75 million in 2005 to just over £5 million by 2008. The ICA's Arts Council grant might have increased by £70,000 between 2006 and 2008, but the most significant change was in the generation of sponsorship income. In 2006 total sponsorship amounted to £306,000. In 2007 this leapt to £970,000. (It was also in early 2007 that the ICA sold off its Picasso mural to the Wellcome Trust for £250,000.) And in 2008 the ICA made £756,000 in sponsorship.

Such large increases were achieved by a new sponsorship led policy, hiring new development and marketing staff tasked with developing high profile sponsorship events that prioritised the ICA 'brand' as a whole, rather than supporting any individual programming department. Not surprisingly, the ICA's wage bill in the period ballooned, from £1.75 million in 2005 to £2.5 million in 2008, although the ICA's accounts report an increase in average staff headcount of only 13. The number of staff paid more than £50,000 rose from three to ten in that period.

If the ICA was riding high on the sponsorship gravy train, more non-programming staff and bigger salaries for those at the top, this was based on marketing projects increasingly untethered from the ICA's core programme content, but instead plugged in to a newer, 'hipper' notion of the ICA as an arbiter of contemporary cool, all the while attempting to harness the spend power of celebrity, and the success-by-association of a heightened media profile. Instead of raising income for the projects of particular departments – Cinema, Exhibitions, Live and Media Arts, and Talks – all energies became focused on 'general projects' drawing big cheques from big corporates. In 2007, a Sony PSP hook-up generated £95,000, a deal with 3G mobile netted £150,000, and the Sony Ericsson backed image anthology and contest All Tomorrow's Pictures earned the ICA £228,000. By 2007, ICA Development had initiated the annual celeb-driven charity auction gala night Figures of Speech. The 2008 edition, attended by such art world luminaries as Nigella Lawson, Tom Dixon and Elle McPherson, rang up £126,000 in the process.

Such sponsorship arrangements are inherently fast burning and short term. Particularly alarming, in this regard, has been the involvement of a more unstable variety of business partners for the ICA's sponsorship projects, and the closeness of those businesses to the ICA's governing council. In 2008 and 2009, the Figures of Speech gala was sponsored by troubled voicemail-to-text message dotcom startup SpinVox. In 2008, SpinVox paid £128,000 for its association with the gala night. While no figures are yet published for the March 2009 edition (also in association with SpinVox), press details released by the ICA record auction results of £86,000, but refer to a headline figure of £180,000 raised by the event, suggesting a similar involvement by SpinVox.

By summer 2009, the £100 million start-up had run out of cash. In December, it was sold to American speech-recognition company Nuance for £64 million. SpinVox's vice-president for consumer business is James Scroggs. Scroggs was also listed as one of the board of directors of the ICA company, appointed in September 2006.

Equally unfortunate was the sponsorship involvement of GuestInvest, the buy-to-let hotel property investor (slogan: 'earn money while others sleep') which had paid £88,000 for a project called ICA TV: London Now, branded ICA video content for hotel TVs. GuestInvest went into administration in October 2008. Its CEO was Johnny Sandelson, who was also a member of the ruling council of the ICA and one of the directors, appointed in October 2007, and who resigned in October 2008. GuestInvest still owes the ICA £33,000.

There are other mistakes not due to the recession. The incautious decision, in September 2008, not long before the Lehman Brothers collapse and the start of the credit crunch proper, to abolish the day membership fee put a further squeeze on income. Sources suggest that the abolition of day membership may have accounted for at least £120,000 in lost revenue to the ICA. And with the abolition of the day-membership, annual membership subscriptions are reported to have declined significantly during 2009.

The picture that emerges is of an organisation in which costs inflated against projected income, based on a marketing model framed by increasingly unrealistic income projections, which left the ICA more exposed to the peculiarly erratic and hard to sustain income streams derived from the marketing budgets of big corporates, the quickly exhausted favour of professional contacts among directors, and the fickle interest of celebrity benefactors. Quite how exposed the ICA became by early 2009 is not clear, but the general experience of the marketing and advertising staff, especially those dealing with brand sponsorship, suggests that many marketing budgets evaporated as brands panicked as the credit crunch hit in earnest in late 2008. But already in early 2008, Mark Sladen, director of exhibitions, was reportedly furious at the Development department's failure to secure any substantial sponsorship for the sixtieth anniversary exhibitions programme 'Nought to Sixty', which ran from May to October 2008. The season culminated with a 60th anniversary auction of work. But with the credit crunch, the game was already over and the auction raised £673,000, failing to realise the £1.3m the ICA had hoped for. Public commitments that revenue from the ICA auction should help establish a commissioning fund for emerging artists were quietly shelved, the proceeds instead directed into the ICA's general funds. Between deluded projections of high-risk income and the undermining of core revenue streams, it may have been a 'perfect storm', but someone was sailing the ship towards it.

There is another term to describe the process occurring in this new 'decentred' art centre – 'de-skilling'

But like Gordon Brown's attitude to his handling of the British economy prior to the recession, Eshun seems convinced that he bears no responsibility for the ICA's recent trajectory, nor its media-dazzled artistic policy, and is now the best person to come to its rescue. Indeed, it seems that for Eshun, Yentob and perhaps secretly even the Arts Council, the financial crisis at the ICA offers an ideal opportunity to spin the current troubles into a story of renewal, with Eshun at the helm. After all, one of the criticisms regularly levelled at the ICA by hostile critics is that the institution is 'no longer relevant'.

Eshun is the ICA's own best critic, of course. At the 10 December meeting, he repeated his mantra that 'all multi-arts spaces are re-thinking what they need to do. The post-war modernist presentation of art is no longer relevant and the ICA needs a vision for what this means.'

Eshun's 'vision' has been long in coming. In a 'vision' document circulated in Spring 2009, Eshun wrote that a key challenge for the ICA was how it might 'update the traditional model of the arts centre with its silo-like programming structure.' The new vision was to be one of fluidity, flexibility, spontaneity and itinerant programming, taking its cue from the model of biennials, fairs and festivals, each of which offered 'a more fluid and decentred model of arts presentation with a focus on new commissions.' The ICA could 'occasionally work in a similar spirit, reconfiguring ourselves as a sometime festival, a freeform space of artistic exploration dedicated to articulating a particular mood or movement.'

But what does updating the 'silo-like' programming structure of the arts centre and seeking a 'more fluid and decentred model of arts presentation' actually mean in practice? One might argue that Eshun's antagonism towards the 'post-war modernist art centre' would seem to run contrary to the ICA's 1947 founding charitable objects:

> To promote the education of the community by encouraging the understanding, appreciation and development of the arts generally and particularly of contemporary art as expressed in painting, etching, engraving, drawing, poetry, philosophy, literature, drama, music, opera, ballet, sculpture, architecture, designs, photography, films, radio and television of educational and cultural value.

Of course, a set of artistic designations as antique as these needs periodic updating; nor does it prescribe the form or structure an organisation should take to deliver such a programme. But Eshun's fascination with the temporary, the flexible and the decentred, of a cultural outlook in which nothing is permanent, was translated into a managerial policy of wearing down the 'silo-like' departmental programming structure of the organisation, at the cost of a loss of curatorial expertise. In October 2008, Eshun decided to abolish the ICA's Live and Media Arts department, a decision which drew acrimonious responses by practitioners in the live and media arts community. And with the resignation of the Talks department in December 2009, increasingly, the responsibility for any original programming fell to exhibitions, the only programming department to have enjoyed any significant budget increase under Eshun's directorship.

'All that matters is now'

There is of course another term to describe the process occurring in this new 'decentred' art centre. It is 'de-skilling'. The vision of a fluid, flexible, temporary institution is, ironically, entirely concomitant with a general trend towards bureaucratisation and the abolition of expertise in organisational structures that mediate between cultural practitioners and arts policy. This has been vividly evident in the changes in arts funding bodies in recent years. For example, the removal of art-form specific advisory panels was an early innovation at Arts Council England under New Labour. A similar process destroyed the British Council's artistic departments in late 2007, when it disbanded its film, drama, dance, literature, design and visual arts departments, amalgamating them into a single 'arts team', organised around bizarre management aphorisms such as 'Progressive Facilitation', 'Market Intelligence Network', 'Knowledge Transfer Function' and 'Modern Pioneer'. In both organisations, the political instinct has been bureaucratic; to withdraw authority and independence from staff appointed for their knowledge of a particular field of artistic practice, in order to better administer whatever policy imperative happens to be coming from central government.

But the hostility of bureaucrats to independent cultural expertise can also be mapped onto the apparently cutting-edge curatorial privileging of flexible, ad hoc programming, and both have the same useful managerial outcomes: fewer staff and more precarious, temporary employment contracts. The disdain for expertise within arts policy thinking also reflects a cynical lack of commitment to the independence of cultural forms, a trivialising indifference to the value those forms have achieved, and an obsession with the mobile tastes of 'the public' as the final arbiter of cultural value. In Eshun's hyperventilating vision document he asks which 'faces should most accurately represent the ICA now?' He concludes:

> It should be the artistic figures that our audience admires... We should celebrate them in our communications as our heroes, our star names *already*, because our audience believes they are cool. And we should keep in mind that in a week to a year hence, many of those figures will no longer be relevant because there will be a new set or more urgent names to hail. All that matters is now.

With a rate of artistic redundancy as fast as this, you don't need curatorial expertise, or an opinion regarding what art is worth supporting and championing – you just need Simon Cowell.

Such abdication of curatorial authority to the audience presupposes that what the audience wants is merely what the institution should do. It does not acknowledge that a presenting institution such as the ICA might have a relationship to communities of artistic practice that have distinct cultural and organisational histories, and their own attendant audiences. Such distinctions cannot simply be wished away by a bit of re-imagineering of a cultural mission statement. If the artistic relevance of the ICA has reputedly dwindled during Eshun's tenure, it perhaps has something to do with how an emptied-out model of audience feedback and 'early-adopter' trend-following became a substitute for agenda-setting, or a critical vision of the current state of art and culture, or real artistic-curatorial relationships with different artistic and cultural communities.

This is not an argument against 'cross-disciplinarity', but it is an argument for the fact that 'cross-disciplinarity' requires the reality of a disciplinary base for practice in the first instance. Forms of artistic creativity are not in constant flux or transformation (though they do change historically) but coalesce into sustained practices and communities of artists and audiences. This is not an outdated 'mode' of the 'post-war modernist art centre', but a recognition that a venue may play host to multiple artistic cultures and communities, which it is not wholly instrumental in generating and sustaining. By contrast, the tendency to abolish programming departments rids an organisation of staff with expertise and commitment to particular fields of activity. It is a move which denies the autonomy of different artistic fields as they already exist outside of the institution, and turns the institution's role from that of forum and enabler for those communities, to a regulator of which artistic practice gains visibility. In other words, it reduces the claim that communities of artistic practitioners can make on cultural institutions, and elevates the institution's arbitrary power over artists by distancing itself from already present communities of practice.

For fans of grotesque irony, The Reading Group outline is unmatched reading

Eshun's blithe comment at the time the closure of the Live and Media Arts department – that new media-based arts practice 'lacks cultural urgency' – is indicative of this confusion between fluid, non-disciplinary notions of curatorial agency, trend-setter indifference to anything that is not 'now' and the bureaucratic tendency to withdraw from contacts with practitioners. It wasn't that there wasn't a lively culture of artistic work being done in live and media arts at the time, but

Image: Ekow Eshun at the AmbITion roadshow, Sadler's Wells Theatre, 16th July, 2009

simply that a cultural director had passed judgement that it was no longer relevant. But such an approach is not surprising; Eshun's previous jobs were as editor of the now defunct *Arena*, the men's style magazine, and before that assistant editor of the equally defunct *The Face*. Observing, selecting, picking-and-mixing, schmoozing the culture in the name of what's cool one moment and not cool the next, are the necessary attributes of mass-media cultural commentators and style arbiters. But they comprise an outlook at odds with negotiating a more complex relationship between artists and the support an institution can bring. The 'flexible institution' is in fact one detached from any relationship of commitment to the art-form communities it has a mission, in part, to represent.

There is another twist to the ICA's current crisis. Prior to the staff meeting of 10 December, the exhibitions department had organised a day-long meeting of invited artists and curators, to discuss a proposed emergency programme project with the working title of the The Reading Group:

> From May 2010 to April 2011 the ICA will undertake an experiment in de-institutionalisation, prototyping a lightweight, responsive arts organisation able to cope with more straitened and complicated times. This will be a time-limited project, exactly a year in duration, during which period the ICA will cease many of its regular activities, and instead play host to a temporary research forum or think tank, addressing a range of urgent questions.

The Reading Group, declared a draft outline of the project, is 'designed to create a space where artists, writers, thinkers and others can come together, share research and work collaboratively, taking the model of The Reading Group as an ideal for temporary communal investigation.'

With the ICA facing one of the most serious financial crises in its 63-year existence, its programme for the next year appears to be a radical-sounding 'experiment in de-institutionalisation', with radical artists and academics co-opted to provide content on a shoestring budget. For fans of grotesque irony The Reading Group outline is unmatched reading; couched in the contemporary terminology of anti-capitalism and art-institutional critique, The Reading Group is slated to address several themes, including 'What work can we do?' (investigating 'alternative ways of thinking about production and labour'), and 'How can we act collectively?' (exploring 'the role of institutions such as the ICA in enabling communal action.') A wish list of cutting-edge artists and academics including Antonio Negri, Hito Steyerl and Eyal Weizman suggests the tenor of the programme.

The Reading Group meeting was attended by a number of curators from European institutions, among them Amsterdam's De Appel, Barcelona's MACBA and Antwerp's Objectif. As one London attendee put it, the general tone of the meeting was always to see questions of financial crisis as an opportunity for a radicalised programme and an opportunity to get 'back to basics'.

Such 'hairshirt radicalism' is common to the confused cultural response to the broader economic crisis. So much of the 'critical' art world has spent the last decade decrying the market boom that it now seems to see the recession as a sort of degraded Marxian 'comeuppance' for the apparent excesses of western consumer capitalism. Because of the general distaste with which 'commodity' art has been held during the boom, it seems those practices which spent the boom decrying the venality of market-driven art, might now be eagerly co-opted as useful filler for institutions no longer able to sustain more costly public programmes. Talk is cheap after all, as are galleries full of tables and chairs, stuff to read and endless discussions to be had about radical projects, conducted by unpaid artists. But as The Reading Group attendee suggested, the only radical discussion not on the table was the only one worth having – how did we get here?

But the crisis at the ICA should be a banal one – it is about dumb financial issues, even dumber management and a precarious and delusional faith in the frothy economics of the boom-time 'creative industries'. Pretending that it is, now, a crisis in the ideological and cultural form of the institution is to provide cultural bureaucrats at ACE and the DCMS with the mission statement to justify the down-sizing and overhaul of all other cultural institutions that run into trouble, while diverting the discussion from the broader politics of the recession. The governing council of the ICA is apparently '100% behind' Eshun. The Arts Council appears to support the current situation, declaring that it accepts

> that the board and management have to make tough and potentially unpopular decisions if the ICA is going to become a sustainable organisation delivering strong artistic programmes, through a fit for purpose organisational structure and robust financial strategy.

The final decision on the release of the second half of the Sustain grant falls to the national council of ACE, though ACE strenuously insists that Eshun's membership of the national council will have no bearing on the decision.

But what of the staff of the ICA who stand to lose most in this debacle? Do they support Eshun? In early February, the staff council called a vote of no confidence in Eshun, but in a bizarre twist, the staff were called to vote on *whether the vote of no confidence should be counted*. The ICA denies that a vote of no confidence has taken place. Five years, it seems, is not long enough for Eshun's first 'experiment in de-institutionalisation'.

JJ Charlesworth <jjcharlesworth@artreview.com> is a freelance critic and associate editor of *ArtReview* magazine

AN END WITHOUT END: CATASTROPHE CINEMA IN THE AGE OF CRISIS

Dusting off the tedium and ash deposited by Hollywood's recent spate of catastrophe movies, Evan Calder Williams takes aim at their world-affirming pessimism and calls for some real apocalypse

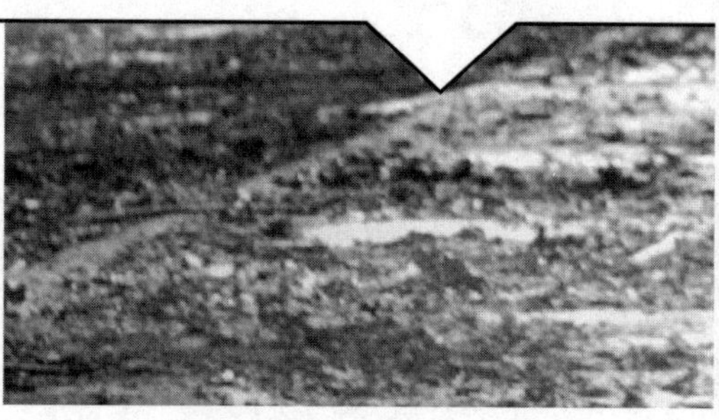

We're in an unprecedented historical moment: if the world should end tomorrow, whatever way it all comes tumbling down will not surprise us in the least. That won't lessen the horror of it, to be sure. Quite the opposite, it will induce the slow-motion gut-sinking realisation 'wait, I've seen this before, and I know all too well how this ends...' For we really have *seen* it before, like never before possible – not a faint premonition or an imminent eschatological prophecy, neither just a dusty woodcut of the whore of Babylon riding into town, nor well-trodden saga lines rolling out Ragnarök and its wolfish aftermath. No, we have the death of the world in full-color and Dolby Stereo, stretched out over thousands of hours. (Even if the colour range is heavily skewed toward ash-grey filtres bathed in damp blue light, and even if the vast majority of those hours is basically interchangeable.)

Hollywood, and the more minor Hollywoods of the globe, have made sure of this and supplied all possible antagonists, from the a-human (asteroids, climate

change, Mayan prophecy, robots, piles of garbage) to the inhuman (zombies, vampires, evil angels, dark underbelly of Hobbesian human nature untethered from the state) to the human (the modern world as somehow responsible for causing nearly all of these possible options). Above all, we have the landscape after the fact: dusty, icy, flooded, bloodied, ruined, voided, burnt, abandoned, misused, and stretched out for us to pore over, even as the sheer excess pours over us.

Call them end-of-the-world movies or post-apocalyptic films, doomsday or disaster cinema. Regardless, we are called by them, insistently, now more so than ever before in mainstream film history: *The Road*, *2012*, *Terminator Salvation*, *Legion*, *Daybreakers*, *Zombieland*, *28 Weeks Later*, *Wall-E*, *Avatar*, *Book of Eli*, to name

Image: still from *The Road*, directed by John Hillcoat, 2009 but a few of the best known recent crop. The tagline for Roland Emmerich's latest orgy of CGI-destruction and pathos-mining, 2009's exceptionally mediocre *2012* is, 'Who Will Be Left Behind?' The answer seems to be, unfortunately, not us. We don't seem to have any choice in that matter – we're along for the ride, for better or largely worse, and frankly we're becoming weary of it.

What persists is the constitutive absence of the new, the unending twilight of more of the same old shit

Because what's at stake here isn't just the rabbit-breeding frequency and quantity of doom and gloom films popping up of late. It's also the accompanying frenzy of wearied attempts by critics, pundits and, perhaps above all, the advertising of the films themselves to *periodise*, to produce accounts and assertions of how these movies are not-so-coded symptoms of our seeming endgame. In short, in the era of severe and protracted financial crisis and global recession, we apparently go to the movies to see a hyperbolic equivalent of the everyday and its looming collapse. Or in other words, all critics become Marxists, if only for a day, straying onto the uncertain terrain of thinking the relation that links the defaulting base to the Armageddon-obsessed superstructure.

The range – from political axe-grinding to sharp, critical thinking – encompassed by these attempts is too wide to cross here, and not particularly important. Of more relevance are two fundamental assumptions that underpin such a tendency:

1. Cultural imaginings of the end of the world serve to 'make sense' of a shared sense of a collapsing world order, the root of which is a massive crisis of global capitalism.
2. It is because we are in that massive financial crisis – and because Hollywood is responding to our taste for apocalyptic imaginings – that we are seeing this current rash of end of the world movies.

What follows, then, is a brief attempt to elaborate the first assumption while fully rejecting the second. In so doing, it is possible to trouble the general sense we have of a discernible correspondence between produced cultural objects, the historical moment of their 'consumption', and the wider political and economic conjuncture from which they indeed cannot be decoupled. To understand what it means to be marked by one's time without being a product of it, perhaps to 'lag ahead'. To try and conceive of what happens when we've hit apocalypse cinema overload too early, before the full

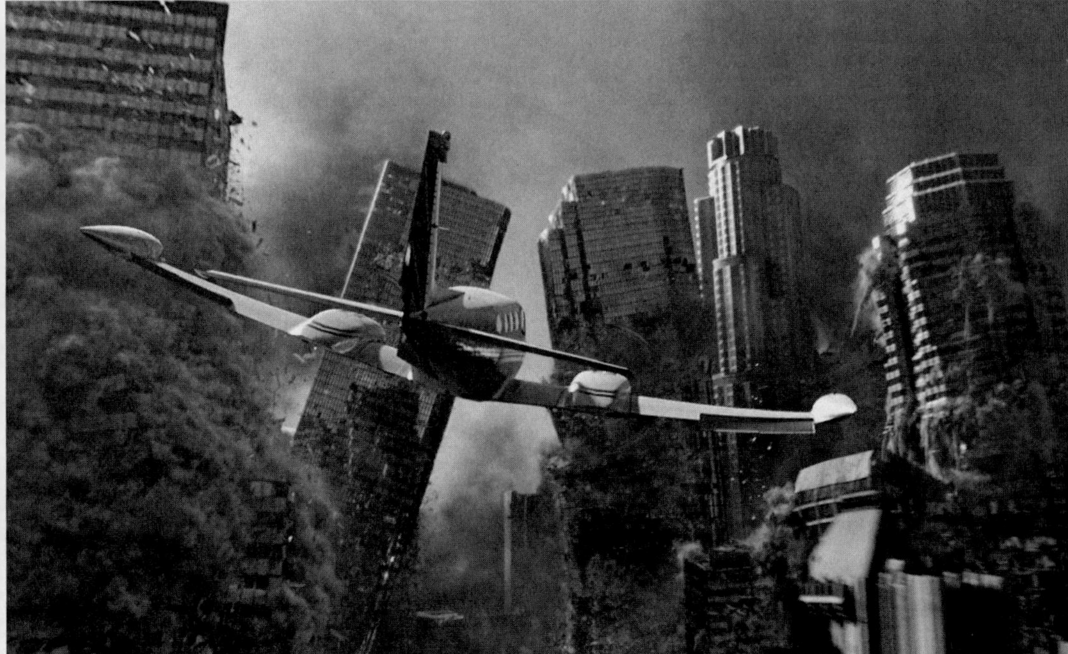

Image: still from *2012*, directed by Roland Emmerich, 2009

consequences of the crisis and its shakedown are felt. And finally, to consider how to pass from a catastrophic popular cinema of stagnant collapse to an apocalyptic popular cinema of refusal, without having to refuse either *cinema* or the *popular*.

To start, we should give some sharpness to how we talk about the end of the world. More specifically, about the difference between a 'crisis', a 'catastrophe', and an 'apocalypse'.

A crisis, in Marxist analysis, does not just signify flagging profitability or the sudden popping of speculative bubbles. Rather, it is the moment when fundamental disequilibrium is violently corrected, when all that 'normally' appeared to be autonomous and independent spheres of the reproduction of the capitalism system, are wrenched back into unity. In our contemporary moment, the unstable gap between the staggering, deleveraged heights of fictitious capital and the 'real world' of fixed capital, material production, and capacity for employment – the gap that made such heights of finance possible in the first place – was abruptly closed. Credit contracted, the naturalised profitability of the future disintegrated, and the wounded totality could be glimpsed, if only for a halted moment.

Image: still from *Avatar*, directed by James Cameron, 2009

In its deeper eschatological roots, *krisis* is a judgement and a separation, the moment that allows the stakes of the battle to appear with clarity. But under capitalism, crisis is not the guarantor of such a reckoning. It is a cyclical, expected and necessary expression, not a permanent state of affairs. It will pass, and be passed through, clearing out systemic dead wood along the way. And it is not an end in itself. A crisis might be read as threatening times of non-recovery to come, but those are the times when it can no longer be called a 'crisis'.

If crisis is a revelation (of contradiction) without the world's end, catastrophe is an end without revelation, an end of the road which doesn't point anywhere beyond itself, just to a historical void. Worse, if it does point somewhere, it is to a post-world that is nostalgic and scrambling to shore up the remnants of its outmoded status quo. Catastrophe looms heavy these days, and not just in the fears of global warming, flu pandemic, or peak oil. The general contraction and decline of late capitalism into its sickly, frantic state very well may become, over the coming decades, *statically* catastrophic. Earlier, in the coalescing moments of the world order now in danger of collapse, champions of neoliberalism and punks alike declared, with varying degrees of cheerfulness, there was *no future*: just the eternal present of this world declaring itself to be the only show in town, even as it veered into war and off the rails. The situation to come is a different *no future*, the slow entropic loss of energy and profit, coupled with the state's brutal refusals – and ways of demanding the same of its citizens and subjects – to acknowledge that the eternal present has become an eternal past.

Lastly, apocalypse, or the 'lifting of the veil'. Apocalypse is an end with revelation. Or rather, it is neither the end of the world nor the revelation that declares and accompanies the end of the world. It is the end of a world order and a way of ordering the world anew. What was there all along, hidden in plain sight, surges into visibility and threatens the organisation of knowledge within which it could not be grasped. In this way, apocalypse is not a terminus, it is an opening, a wound that will not close, the revelation of what was there but not acknowledged. Crucially, the apocalypse makes possible the hard work of the post-apocalypse, of reordering not a dead world, but a world into which has erupted what doesn't belong. Which is to say, under capitalism, all that is needed to make it all run but which must continually be shoved out of sight: masses of the dispossessed, bare coercion behind the market, requisite creative destruction, increasingly unstable ecosystems, the basic antagonism of work itself, everything that is without value.

krisis is a judgment and a separation, the moment that allows the stakes of the battle to appear with clarity

Casually, we talk about the majority of these films as 'post-apocalyptic'.[1] But for the most part we are talking about a world in which either the end has already come (i.e. dystopian landscape-traversing survivors) or in which it won't stop coming (i.e. zombies). However, we should really speak of them as part of a 'cinema of catastrophe', in which the emphasis is not on what is revealed but on a world-collapsing end without difference, but also without end. The world may be destroyed, but it neither goes away nor opens wounds of possibility. What persists is the constitutive absence of the new, the unending twilight of more of the same old shit. The eventual rupture of history becomes a termination, above all, of the whole fantasy of civilisational progress. We're left with the bled-out present hobbling forward, dragging along its raggedy caravan of outmoded social forms, and muttering to itself.

However, we get ahead of ourselves. The central issue here is the intuitive notion that the current overgrown batch of imagined ends, entropic or abrupt, is a response to a changing economic situation and to the real anxieties engendered by what may come with a deepening financial crisis that signals catastrophe for global capitalism's future health and the livelihoods of the vast majority who live within it.

Unfortunately, this isn't the case, at least in any direct way, for the simple reason of how movies are made. 'Culture' may necessarily lag behind shifts in the economic base, but mainstream film provides a more concrete lag that nearly defangs a simultaneist-materialist correspondence theory of culture. Big budget movies take a very long time to go from concept to screen. For all intents and purposes, September 2008 was when the current crisis hit mass awareness, inaugurating the months of bank closures, bailouts, and massive credit default. What of our catastrophic cinema? When did their concepts – and hence the broad shape of their 'reflection' of the crisis – come to be? A quick breakdown:

these films reveal the anxiety of static catastrophe, the end with its foreclosed possibility of starting over differently

– *Wall-E* (2008): concept developed in 1994, in the works since
– *2012* (2009): script finished and marketed in Feb 2008
– *Terminator Salvation* (2009): concept first drafted in1999, film finished in summer 2008
– *The Road* (2009): screenplay adapted in April 2007 (from a 2006 novel), filming began in February 2008
– *Avatar* (2009): based on a 1994 script treatment and in the digital works for many years thereafter
– *Daybreakers* (2010): shooting finished in September 2007
– *Legion* (2010): principal photography in summer 2008
– *Book of Eli* (2010): Hughes Brothers signed on in May 2007 to an already written script

Barring a theory focused on how the editing, marketing, and minor aesthetic choices of these films were determined by economic disaster, these films cannot be reflections of either the crisis at its most visible or of consequent consumer anxiety. The films claimed as symptomatic of our current worries about global financial collapse were in fact made before the crisis broke.

Given that my point is obviously not to discard materialist readings of culture, a few options – all of which say these are not 'crisis films' – point a way forward:

1. These are prescribed films that would have been made regardless of the economic situation
2. These are prescient films that sniffed out what was to come
3. These are pre-crisis films, time capsules from the still-inflating bubbles before
4. These are films of the present, made then under the same conditions that engendered the current crisis, and which therefore parallel its tendencies toward both giganticism and weariness

Our way forward is to say, somewhat paradoxically: all four mutually exclusive descriptions are correct, and it is this over-determination that makes these catastrophic visions real 'crisis films'.

Indeed, Hollywood would have made them anyway. The prior filmography of Emmerich alone, including *Independence Day*, *The Day After Tomorrow*, and *Godzilla*, reminds us that these movies just keep happening as long as they keep bringing in money. And our attempts to see in them a distorted, blown-up nightmare of this crisis seems just that: an attempt, an over-extended reach to suture meaning to contingency. Yet it is this coincidence, that uncanny sense of alignment (financial catastrophe – catastrophic cinema), of a sudden linkage, that makes them films of crisis. In other words, it is because they are not films *of the crisis* that they are crisis films: our yearning glimpse of a totality and feeling that even our entertainment is marked inexorably by the economic, is the experience of crisis and its violent, contracting alignment of everything yoked abstractly together through the circuits of reproduction.

Furthermore, without assigning a zeitgeist bloodhound role to the general intellect of Hollywood, the films do capture something of their time. For the sense of catastrophe wasn't just in the air. The period in which these films were conceived and made coincides with the economic foundation of the 'long downturn', the hugely overdue system-wide crisis of manufacturing and profitability deferred precisely by financial speculation and turbulent bubblenomics. They couldn't help but capture this, and with it, the sense that the crisis is ongoing. Not in the loose Marxism of 'capitalism is crisis', but by providing a glimpse of a longer history that necessarily bleeds toward a wider vista of capital's fundamental, irreconcilable contradictions that won't be perpetually deferred through multiple crises. In short, these films of crisis are *catastrophic cinema*, for they reveal that contemporary capitalism is terminal *catastrophe*, not crisis. That is the promise, rarely elaborated by the films, of their apocalyptic labour of revealing what isn't new, but hidden in plain sight. Namely, the anxiety of the *static catastrophe*, the end that inaugurates only the foreclosed possibility of starting over differently.

And that is the central feeling of these films, which are indeed shaped by their inception in the bubble years. They are marked by the lead-up to crisis, the last years of mad profit and risk before the collapse, when the frayed edges became more visible. The years when capitalism witnessed its own obscene, autophagic repetition, as high finance insistently did what it and everyone else knew to be digging the grave deeper. If such a backdrop didn't concretely inform these films, it may as well have. For if we ask what kind of films they are 'in general', two dominant tendencies of catastrophic cinema come to the fore: they are obsessed with the persistence of what should have gone away – the end of the world didn't get rid of that world; they articulate fears, not of economic failure per se, but of an ongoing disaster of economy itself, of the fundamental impossibility of aligning supplies with needs, of production with consumption, even as they resolutely mourn the lost 'stability' of the doomed late capitalist order.

But when the lights go off, the cannibalistic urge flicks on...

What do we mean? A real survey exceeds our scope here, but we can nevertheless map these tendencies across the major films.

Zombies (*Zombieland*, *28 Weeks Later*, countless other iterations): even in their most smugly self-knowing incarnations, the films – and viral hipster fetish – that has recently ruled the day make literal the non-revelation of catastrophe. They are obscene persistence made manifest, an occasion to witness the cathartic and gory dismantling of bodies that don't know when to die and rot away. For they aren't really about the 'living dead' and never have been. They are about the living who never could die, infected with *surplus-life*, doomed to consumption without hunger. If we speak of zombie 'apocalypse', what lies behind the veil is more of the same, exhausted, necrotic, unable to clock-out from a labour that knows no end.

Robots and Trash (*Wall-E* and *Terminator Salvation*): we don't turn against ourselves, zombie-like, but the rush toward profit and consumption produces constitutive excess that makes us bloated fat milkshake-drinkers in need of robot salvation, or lean, dirty mercenaries in need of salvation from our killer robots. In both cases, we brought it on ourselves, through our inability to manage our waste and our attempts to solve it via high technology. With it, the dazzling world of rubble, too strewn with the remnants of the past to start anew without resetting the clock (*Wall-E*'s back-to-the-Earth primitive resettling, *Terminator Salvation*'s temporal feedback loops).

Earth Threatening Disaster (*2012*, most recently): we may have 'been warned', but what can we do when the cause is solar flares heating the Earth's core? Following one of the more stunning naturalisations of catastrophe (it isn't just beyond our control, it is written into Mayan legend and outer space), it becomes only a question of disaster management and disastrous mismanagement, of too few 'arks' (read: barely veiled stand-in for developed nations) for too many people. What remains is just the full-blown pathos of the remainder, the desperate clutching to the broken timber of the family in the storm, and a gaze onto spectacles of destruction so lusty it becomes near impossible to feel anything other than concomitant shame and arousal.

Vampiric Corporations (*Daybreakers*): almost too allegorical to touch, nearly a missing horror-fantasy written by the young Marx, *Twilight* for anti-capitalists. A corporation supplying the blood of the living to a world of bourgeois vampires? The attempt to circumvent problems of inadequate productivity with biotechnology (synthetic blood substitute)? The ultimate irreconcilability of production with 'unnatural', inhuman hunger for consumption? A consequent nostalgia for older anthropological arrangements as 'better' via the conservative defense of the human (à la *I Am Legend*)? It's high time for the proletariat to out-vampire the ruling class.

Dusty Scarcity (*The Road*): a terrible, terrible film, very serious about being serious, full of Von Trierean sadistic sentimentality without acknowledging it. The basic need of consumption runs up against the causeless collapse of all production, even biological, as all goes grey and plants stop growing. With it, a full nostalgia for the managed consumption of late capitalism, pushing a rickety shopping cart across the country, the reverent hush before the gift of an unopened can of Coke.[2] The dusky prettiness is that of a halted, still, ashen world, in which only recourse to the nuclear family will help us still be 'good guys'. Because, as we all know, in the wake of liberal capitalism's demise, any form of collectivity that isn't familial leads only to the wrong consumption of human flesh, supposedly abhorrent precisely because the need to survive shouldn't disrupt the sanctity of the social contract. But when the lights go off, the cannibalistic urge flicks on…

Lush Excess (*Avatar*): conversely, *Avatar* is possibly the most staggering display of pure plenitude ever committed to the American screen. On what ground does it rest? Underground, a massive deposit of the unobtainable made manifest – the rare 'Unobtanium' metal to be mined. Flowering above, total wet fecundity, illimitable hybrid biopower, interspecies interpenetration, an absence of agriculture or organised production, and trees that have developed an information network for which Google would happily displace many millions of animist, lithe, bare-assed tribes. (What is the wealth of the Unobtanium in the face of all that lush forest and 'technologies of nature' to be explored?) Forget any issues about 'war on terror', liberal guilt, noble savages or the like. It's the full subsumption of politics to the prospect of an era of unbound plenty. It is a cinema of anti-crisis that blows away the very category and possibility of scarcity. A wish-fulfillment of profit and profligacy behind every corner, hanging from every luminescent vine. When each digital fibre drips with such lush excess, what else is there to do but frolic and drool?

Pseudo-Christian End (*Legion* and *Book of Eli*): The most recent catastrophic films have taken a definite turn for the explicitly Christian: God decides to destroy the world, Denzel Washington carries a Braille Bible to get the post-apocalypse back on track in what can only be described as *The Road* plus martial arts plus the church. But in both cases, as with *2012*, they lack the courage to lay bare their eschatology. We'd prefer a full CGI-covered 'Book of Revelations' to this, when *Legion*'s God lacks the gumption to follow through on the apocalypse (or the infinite resources to do it himself without passing the buck to his angels). What's notable, therefore, isn't the fact of a Christian perspective but its remobilisation toward other ends. In this way, these are flawless apologists for crisis and for the way forward through the reenactment of the same under slightly different names. A reactionary cinema of adaptive non-advance, they merely rescript the already given and morbidly persistent beneath a slightly more heterodox and ethical star.

To conclude, we should ask: what now? As the financial crisis continues, will we see films marked by the anxieties proper to the full visibility – and material effects – of its unfolding? Will we get a genuinely apocalyptic, rather than merely catastrophic, cinema? If the past is any indication, no. Even if the crisis produces a systemic contraction of the film-attending purchase power of consumers, as in the Great Depression studio shakeout, these movies will hardly be the first to go. Furthermore, even if culture doesn't necessarily 'lag' behind real world conditions, the culture industry certainly does: it'll be damned if it adapts. Zombies, floods, and trash-sorting robots don't appear because they 'stand in' for the economy, and they won't disappear because the economy gets worse. We may think we're past the point of catastrophe film saturation, but we ain't seen nothing yet.

it isn't just beyond our control, it is written into Mayan legend and outer space

Image: still from *Terminator: Salvation,* directed by McG, 2009

In short, if we want apocalypse, not catastrophe, during this time of crisis, we can't look to Hollywood. Apocalypse is not the subject matter of 'The End': it is a position of revelation without transcendence, of making unmistakable what we've disavowed for too long. The particularity of cinema in the age of crisis is in *how* viewers relate to it. It isn't those imagined trajectories of the world order's collapse that is particular to crisis, but the desperate searching itself. So for us to call for an apocalyptic cinema is to call solely for a combative, striving post-apocalyptic stance in relation to the catastrophe that is contemporary capitalism and its films. It is in the degree to which we neither sit and weep because Daddy is dying nor drool because everything is illuminated, but rather start to sift, sort, and scrap, to ask what we can use and what should be rejected in full. A post-apocalyptic cinema is not a kind of film: it is a kind of space, an urgent diagonal cut to be made across the futile stagnancy of the day, a reclamation of the ruins, a refusal that neither flees nor abandons.

Footnotes

1 For those that involve big waves and bigger displays of sentimentality, we usually reserve the specificity of 'disaster movies' or 'doomsday scenarios'.

2 And, as China Miéville has pithily put it in a McSweeney's review, regarding the death of the father at the end of their journey: 'In that shopless nightmare, what else is afflicting him but consumption?'

Evan Calder Williams <evancalder@gmail.com> is a theorist and graduate student in Santa Cruz, California. His book, *Combined and Uneven Apocalypse,* will be published by Zero Books in fall 2010. His blog is http://socialismandorbarbarism.blogspot.com

APOCALYPSE, TENDENCY, CRISIS

Crises tend to generate apocalyptic dreams and nightmares. Through a reappraisal of 20th century anti-capitalist thought, Benjamin Noys urges us to critically re-think how such an apocalyptic tone operates within radical analyses of the current crisis

In a time of crisis apocalyptic desires and fantasies become pressing and real.[1] Norman Cohn's *In Pursuit of the Millennium* (1957) offers a secret history of the periodic emergence of a 'revolutionary eschatology' in the Middle Ages in response to a collapsing social order, immiseration, disease and war. Responding to crisis these dreamers dared to imagine an apocalypse that would turn the world upside down, and create a new heaven on earth in which princes would bow to peasants. Of course the apocalypse that became real was often the apocalypse of repression. The repression in the wake of the Peasants' War in Germany (1524-26) led to the deaths of over 100,000 peasants, and the eventual execution of its leader Thomas Müntzer who, under torture, proclaimed '*Omnia sunt communia*' (All things are to be held in common). Cohn, an anti-communist liberal, regarded these millenarians as dangerous forerunners of the 'totalitarian' movements of the 20th century and, in the 1970 edition, extended this to condemn '60s counter culture by linking these medieval proto-anarchists to Charles Manson's death cult. Of course, the Situationists would deliberately re-purpose Cohn, reclaiming these rebels from 'the condescension of posterity', to use E. P. Thompson's famous phrase.[2] Apocalyptic desires are ambiguous, at once consolatory fantasies, deferred hopes and, potentially, spurs to radical re-orderings.

We are living in a time of crisis and potential apocalypse, with the overlapping of the financial crisis, ecological crisis and the crisis of movements of resistance. The apocalyptic imagination feeds on this to produce dreams or nightmares of a world

PROUD TO BE FLESH

A MUTE MAGAZINE ANTHOLOGY OF CULTURAL POLITICS AFTER THE NET

Edited by Josephine Berry Slater and Pauline van Mourik Broekman

ARTS COUNCIL
ENGLAND

MUTE

All images by "   " [sic] TIM GOLDIE

'cleansed' of humanity, from *2012* to the History Channel's *Life After People*. These fundamentally reactionary fantasies can only imagine redemption of our fallen world on the condition that humanity ceases to exist, or is reduced to the 'right' number of the 'saved'. What concerns me here is thinking more closely the relation between radical and revolutionary thought and an 'apocalyptic tone' in our current context. The usual model of such a tone was proposed by Kant, when he argued that it was the result of the illegitimate extension of reason beyond its limits towards a transcendent 'exalted vision' (*schwärmerische Vision*).[3] Failing to recognise the limits of reality the apocalyptic dreamer was a fanatic (*schwärmerei*) trying to impose an abstract vision on reality.[4] I am more interested in another version of this apocalyptic tone, one which is generated by a claimed *immanence* of thought to reality.

In this case apocalypse is not generated by some external superior transcendent vision but by the immanent tendencies of the present. This is a tone which remains within, if often heretically, the ambit of Marxism. Marx famously riposted to Proudhon that history advances by the 'bad side', and, writing with Engels in *The Communist Manifesto*, that class struggle would each time end 'either in a revolutionary reconstitution of society at large, or in the common ruin of the contending classes'.[5] I'm not concerned with the old Cold War trope that Marxism is really a form of religion with its own eschatology. I am, however, critiquing the remnants of a religious model of providence, in which we suppose history is necessarily on our side. In particular I want to problematise the radicalisation of Marx's argument that suggests if history advances by the 'bad side' then the worse things get, the better the potential results. In the context of the current crisis we can think of those who argue the need to radicalise and deepen the tendencies that led to the crisis, which includes Franco 'Bifo' Berardi's contention that the current crisis is actually the demise of capitalism under the pressure 'of the potency of productive forces (cognitive labour in the global network)'; the claim by Angela Mitropolous and Melinda Cooper that the crisis is generated by 'usury from below ... that extended beyond the limits which were tolerable to capital'; and Antonio Negri's argument that 'no New Deal is possible', and so we must go on to more radical demands.[6]

The apocalyptic imagination feeds on crisis to produce dreams of a world 'cleansed' of humanity

Of course all these thinkers are trying to call for a new inventiveness in the face of crisis and resisting, rightly I think, the usual calls for sacrifice and austerity – calls which usually fall on the victims of the crisis rather than those who caused it. That said they also imply that by a kind of radical or quasi-Marxist 'cunning of reason' the very worst will produce the 'good', or at least the moment of choice between 'the revolutionary reconstitution of society at large' and 'the common ruin of contending classes.' What they also share is a remarkably traditional and teleological, if not providential, model of the dialectic between the forces and relations of production, in which, to cite Marx from the 1859 Preface,

> the material productive forces of society come into conflict with the existing relations of production ... [and] [f]rom forms of development of the productive forces these relations turn into their fetters. Then begins an era of social revolution.[7]

Transforming the 'productive forces' into the powers of the multitude or the cognitariat carries the implication that the crisis will deliver its own radical solution, or, again to return to the 1859 Preface, that

> Mankind thus inevitably sets itself only such tasks as it is able to solve, since closer examination will always show that the problem itself arises only when the material conditions for its solution are already present or at least in the course of formation.[8]

I want to problematise this 'apocalyptic tone' by returning to the Marxist concept of the tendency, and by suggesting the need to complicate the model that the tendencies of the present will deliver the apocalyptic realisation of communism.

The Method of the Tendency

The concept of the tendency makes a key appearance in volume three of *Capital*, with what Gopal Balakrishnan calls Marx's 'notoriously unclear' reflections on 'the tendency of the rate of profit to fall'.[9] Here I do not want to consider the lengthy and vituperative debate on Marx's speculation, but rather to attend to the way in which Marx's remarks on the 'tendency' became re-worked into a method of analysis. Crucial here is Lukács's *History and Class Consciousness* (1923) and his argument, in the central essay on 'Reification and the Consciousness of the Proletariat', that the tendency is the key tool in allowing us to grasp the historical process by dissolving the reified appearance of capital: 'This image of a frozen reality that nevertheless is caught up in an unremitting, ghostly movement at once becomes meaningful when this reality is dissolved into the process of which man is the driving force.'[10] This dissolution of reified appearance means, as Lukács notes, 'that the *developing tendencies of history constitute a higher reality than the empirical "facts"*.'[11]

"HA HA HA HA HA HA HA HA HA HA HA HA HA HA HA HA HA HA HA HA HA HA HA HA HA HA HA HA HA HA HA HA HA HA HA HA HA
HA HA HA HA HA HA HA HA HA HA HA HA HA HA HA HA HA HA HA HA HA HA HA HA HA HA HA HA HA HA HA HA HA HA HA HA HA
HA HA HA HA HA HA HA HA HA HA HA HA HA HA HA HA HA HA HA HA HA HA HA HA HA HA HA HA HA HA HA HA HA HA HA HA HA
HA HA HA HA HA HA HA HA HA HA HA HA HA HA HA HA HA HA HA HA HA HA HA HA HA HA HA HA HA HA HA HA HA HA HA HA HA
HA HA HA HA HA HA HA HA HA HA HA HA HA HA HA HA HA HA HA HA HA HA HA HA HA HA HA HA HA HA HA HA HA HA HA HA HA
HA HA HA HA HA HA HA HA HA HA HA HA HA HA HA HA HA HA HA HA HA HA HA HA HA HA HA HA HA HA HA HA HA HA HA HA HA
HA HA HA HA HA HA HA HA HA HA HA HA HA HA HA HA HA HA HA HA HA HA HA HA HA HA HA HA HA HA HA HA HA HA HA HA HA
HA HA HA HA HA HA HA HA HA HA HA HA HA HA HA HA HA HA HA HA HA HA HA HA HA HA HA HA HA HA HA HA HA HA HA HA HA
HA HA HA HA HA HA HA HA HA HA HA HA HA HA HA HA HA HA HA HA HA HA HA HA HA HA HA HA HA HA HA HA HA HA HA HA HA
HA HA HA HA HA HA HA HA HA HA HA HA HA HA HA HA HA HA HA HA HA HA HA HA HA HA HA HA HA HA HA HA HA HA HA HA HA
HA HA HA HA HA HA HA HA HA HA HA HA HA HA HA HA HA HA HA HA HA HA HA HA HA HA HA HA HA HA HA HA HA HA HA HA HA
HA HA HA HA HA HA HA HA HA HA HA HA HA HA HA HA HA HA HA HA HA HA HA HA HA HA HA HA HA HA HA HA HA HA HA HA HA
HA HA HA HA HA HA HA HA HA HA HA HA HA HA HA HA HA HA HA HA HA HA HA HA HA HA HA HA HA HA HA HA HA HA HA HA HA
HA HA HA HA HA HA HA HA HA HA HA HA HA HA HA HA HA HA HA HA HA HA HA HA HA HA HA HA HA HA HA HA HA HA HA HA HA
HA HA HA HA HA HA HA HA HA HA HA HA HA HA HA HA HA HA HA HA HA HA HA HA HA HA HA HA HA HA HA HA HA HA HA HA HA
HA HA HA HA HA HA HA HA HA HA HA HA HA HA HA HA HA HA HA HA HA HA HA HA HA HA HA HA HA HA HA HA HA HA HA HA HA
HA HA HA HA HA HA HA HA HA HA HA HA HA HA HA HA HA HA HA HA HA HA HA HA HA HA HA HA HA HA HA HA HA HA HA HA HA
HA HA HA HA HA HA HA HA HA HA HA HA HA HA HA HA HA HA HA HA HA HA HA HA HA HA HA HA HA HA HA HA HA HA HA HA HA
HA HA HA HA HA HA HA HA HA HA HA HA HA HA HA HA HA HA HA HA HA HA HA HA HA HA HA HA HA HA HA HA HA HA HA HA HA
HA HA HA HA HA HA HA HA HA HA HA HA HA HA HA HA HA HA HA HA HA HA HA HA HA HA HA HA HA HA HA HA HA HA HA HA HA
HA HA HA HA HA HA HA HA HA HA HA HA HA HA HA HA HA HA HA HA HA HA HA HA HA HA HA HA HA HA HA HA HA HA HA HA HA
HA HA HA HA HA HA HA HA HA HA HA HA HA HA HA HA HA HA HA HA HA HA HA HA HA HA HA HA HA HA HA HA HA HA HA HA HA
HA HA HA HA HA HA HA HA HA HA HA HA HA HA HA HA HA HA HA HA HA HA HA HA HA HA HA HA HA HA HA HA HA HA HA HA HA
HA HA HA HA HA HA HA HA HA HA HA HA HA HA HA HA HA HA HA HA HA HA HA HA HA HA HA HA HA HA HA HA HA HA HA HA HA
HA HA HA HA HA HA HA HA HA HA HA HA HA HA HA HA HA HA HA HA HA HA HA HA HA HA HA HA HA HA HA HA HA HA HA HA HA
HA HA HA HA HA HA HA HA HA HA HA HA HA HA HA HA HA HA HA HA HA HA HA HA HA HA HA HA HA HA HA HA HA HA HA HA HA
HA HA HA HA HA HA HA HA HA HA HA HA HA HA HA HA HA HA HA HA HA HA HA HA HA HA HA HA HA HA HA HA HA HA HA HA HA
HA HA HA HA HA HA HA HA HA HA HA HA HA HA HA HA HA HA HA HA HA HA HA HA HA HA HA HA HA HA HA HA HA HA HA HA HA
HA HA HA HA HA HA HA HA HA HA HA HA HA HA HA HA HA HA HA HA HA HA HA HA HA HA HA HA HA HA HA HA HA HA HA HA HA
HA HA HA HA HA HA HA HA HA HA HA HA HA HA HA HA HA HA HA HA HA HA HA HA HA HA HA HA HA HA HA HA HA HA HA HA HA
HA HA HA HA HA HA HA HA HA HA HA HA HA HA HA HA HA HA HA HA HA HA HA HA HA HA HA HA HA HA HA HA HA HA HA HA HA
HA HA HA HA HA HA HA HA HA HA HA HA HA HA HA HA HA HA HA HA HA HA HA HA HA HA HA HA HA HA HA HA HA HA HA HA HA
HA HA HA HA HA HA HA HA HA HA HA HA HA HA HA HA HA HA HA HA HA HA HA HA HA HA HA HA HA HA HA HA HA HA HA HA HA
HA HA HA HA HA HA HA HA HA HA HA HA HA HA HA HA HA HA HA HA HA HA HA HA HA HA HA HA HA HA HA HA HA HA HA HA HA
HA HA HA HA HA HA HA HA HA HA HA HA HA HA HA HA HA HA HA HA HA HA HA HA HA HA HA HA HA HA HA HA HA HA HA HA HA
HA HA HA HA HA HA HA HA HA HA HA HA HA HA HA HA HA HA HA HA HA HA HA HA HA HA HA HA HA HA HA HA HA HA HA HA HA
HA HA HA HA HA HA HA HA HA HA HA HA HA HA HA HA HA HA HA HA HA HA HA HA HA HA HA HA HA HA HA HA HA HA HA HA HA
HA HA HA HA HA HA HA HA HA HA HA HA HA HA HA HA HA HA HA HA HA HA HA HA HA HA HA HA HA HA HA HA HA HA HA HA HA
HA HA HA HA HA HA HA HA HA HA HA HA HA HA HA HA HA HA HA HA HA HA HA HA HA HA HA HA HA HA HA HA HA HA HA HA HA
HA HA HA HA HA HA HA HA HA HA HA HA HA HA HA HA HA HA HA HA HA HA HA HA HA HA HA HA HA HA HA HA HA HA HA HA HA
HA HA HA HA HA HA HA HA HA HA HA HA HA HA HA HA HA HA HA HA HA HA HA HA HA HA HA HA HA HA HA HA HA HA HA HA HA
HA HA HA HA HA HA HA HA HA HA HA HA HA HA HA HA HA HA HA HA HA HA HA HA HA HA HA HA HA HA HA HA HA HA HA HA HA
HA HA HA HA HA HA HA HA HA HA HA HA HA HA HA HA HA HA HA HA HA HA HA HA HA HA HA HA HA HA HA HA HA HA HA HA HA
HA HA HA HA HA HA HA HA HA HA HA HA HA HA HA HA HA HA HA HA HA HA HA HA HA HA HA HA HA HA HA HA HA HA HA HA HA
HA HA HA HA HA HA HA HA HA HA HA HA HA HA HA HA HA HA HA HA HA HA HA HA HA HA HA HA HA HA HA HA HA HA HA HA HA
HA HA HA HA HA HA HA HA HA HA HA HA HA HA HA HA HA HA HA HA HA HA HA HA HA HA HA HA HA HA HA HA HA HA HA HA HA
HA HA HA HA HA HA HA HA HA HA HA HA HA HA HA HA HA HA HA HA HA HA HA HA HA HA HA HA HA HA HA HA HA HA HA HA HA
HA HA HA HA HA HA HA HA HA HA HA HA HA HA HA HA HA HA HA HA HA HA HA HA HA HA HA HA HA HA HA HA HA HA HA HA HA
HA HA HA HA HA HA HA HA HA HA HA HA HA HA HA HA HA HA HA HA HA HA HA HA HA HA HA HA HA HA HA HA HA HA HA HA HA
HA HA HA HA HA HA HA HA HA HA HA HA HA HA HA HA HA HA HA HA HA HA HA HA HA HA HA HA HA HA HA HA HA HA HA HA HA
HA HA HA HA HA HA HA HA HA HA HA HA HA HA HA HA HA HA HA HA HA HA HA HA HA HA HA HA HA HA HA HA HA HA HA HA HA
HA HA HA HA HA HA HA HA HA HA HA HA HA HA HA HA HA HA HA HA HA HA HA HA HA HA HA HA HA HA HA HA HA HA HA HA HA
HA HA HA HA HA HA HA HA HA HA HA HA HA HA HA HA HA HA HA HA HA HA HA HA HA HA HA HA HA HA HA HA HA HA HA HA HA
HA HA HA HA HA HA HA HA HA HA HA HA HA HA HA HA HA HA HA HA HA HA HA HA HA HA HA HA HA HA HA HA HA HA HA HA HA
HA HA HA HA HA HA HA HA HA HA HA HA HA HA HA HA HA HA HA HA HA HA HA HA HA HA HA HA HA HA HA HA HA HA HA HA HA
HA HA HA HA HA HA HA HA HA HA HA HA HA HA HA HA HA HA HA HA HA HA HA HA HA HA HA HA HA HA HA HA HA HA HA HA HA
HA HA HA HA HA HA HA HA HA HA HA HA HA HA HA HA HA HA HA HA HA HA HA HA HA HA HA HA HA HA HA HA HA HA HA HA HA
HA HA HA HA HA HA HA HA HA HA HA HA HA HA HA HA HA HA HA HA HA HA HA HA HA HA HA HA HA HA HA HA HA HA HA HA HA
HA HA HA HA HA HA HA HA HA HA HA HA HA HA HA HA HA HA HA HA HA HA HA HA HA HA HA HA HA HA HA HA HA HA HA HA HA
HA HA HA HA HA HA HA HA HA HA HA HA HA HA HA HA HA HA HA HA HA HA HA HA HA HA HA HA HA HA HA HA HA HA HA HA HA
HA HA HA HA HA HA HA HA HA HA HA HA HA HA HA HA HA HA HA HA HA HA HA HA HA HA HA HA HA HA HA HA HA HA HA HA HA
HA HA HA HA HA HA HA HA HA HA HA HA HA HA HA HA HA HA HA HA HA HA HA HA HA HA HA HA HA HA HA HA HA HA HA HA HA
HA HA HA HA HA HA HA HA HA HA HA HA HA HA HA HA HA HA HA HA HA HA HA HA HA HA HA HA HA HA HA HA HA HA HA HA HA
HA HA HA HA HA HA HA HA HA HA HA HA HA HA HA HA HA HA HA HA HA HA HA HA HA HA HA HA HA HA HA HA HA HA HA HA HA
HA HA HA HA HA HA HA HA HA HA HA HA HA HA HA HA HA HA HA HA HA HA HA HA HA HA HA HA HA HA HA HA HA HA HA HA HA
HA HA HA HA HA HA HA HA HA HA HA HA HA HA HA HA HA HA HA HA HA HA HA HA HA HA HA HA HA HA HA HA HA HA HA HA HA
HA HA HA HA HA HA HA HA HA HA HA HA HA HA HA HA HA HA HA HA HA HA HA HA HA HA HA HA HA HA HA HA HA HA HA HA HA
HA HA HA HA HA HA HA HA HA HA HA HA HA HA HA HA HA HA HA HA HA HA HA HA HA HA HA HA HA HA HA HA HA HA HA HA HA
HA HA HA HA HA HA HA HA HA HA HA HA HA HA HA HA HA HA HA HA HA HA HA HA HA HA HA HA HA HA HA HA HA HA HA HA HA
HA HA HA HA HA HA HA HA HA HA HA HA HA HA HA HA HA HA HA HA HA HA HA HA HA HA HA HA HA HA HA HA HA HA HA HA HA
HA HA HA HA HA HA HA HA HA HA HA HA HA HA HA HA HA HA HA HA HA HA HA HA HA HA HA HA HA HA HA HA HA HA HA HA HA
HA HA HA HA HA HA HA HA HA HA HA HA HA HA HA HA HA HA HA HA HA HA HA HA HA HA HA HA HA HA HA HA HA HA HA HA HA
HA HA HA HA HA HA HA HA HA HA HA HA HA HA HA HA HA HA HA HA HA HA HA HA HA HA HA HA HA HA HA HA HA HA HA HA HA
HA HA HA HA HA HA HA HA HA HA HA HA HA HA HA HA HA HA HA HA HA HA HA HA HA HA HA HA HA HA HA HA HA HA HA HA HA
HA HA HA HA HA HA HA HA HA HA HA HA HA HA HA HA HA HA HA HA HA HA HA HA HA HA HA HA HA HA HA HA HA HA HA HA HA
HA HA HA HA HA HA HA HA HA HA HA HA HA HA HA HA HA HA HA HA HA HA HA HA HA HA HA HA HA HA HA HA HA HA HA HA HA
HA HA HA HA HA HA HA HA HA HA HA HA HA HA HA HA HA HA HA HA HA HA HA HA HA HA HA HA HA HA HA HA HA HA HA HA HA
HA HA HA HA HA HA HA HA HA HA HA HA HA HA HA HA HA HA HA HA HA HA HA HA HA HA HA HA HA HA HA HA HA HA HA HA HA
HA HA HA HA HA HA HA HA HA HA HA HA HA HA HA HA HA HA HA HA HA HA HA HA HA HA HA HA HA HA HA HA HA HA HA HA" [sic]

The tendency or tendencies therefore have a particularly tricky form – a dialectical form in fact – in which 'the objective forms of the objects are themselves transformed into a process, a flux.'[12] This 'flux' is no Bergsonian 'duration' (*durée réelle*), which is merely 'vacuous' according to Lukács, but a tracing of the 'unbroken production and reproduction of ... [social] relations'.[13] Of course the tension is that such a dissolution of the (reified) 'facts' can easily be regarded as mere speculation detached from reality, which is often the way in which the dialectic has been taken by bourgeois thought and even by certain forms of Marxism. Lukács recognises that this is a 'theory of reality which allots a higher place to the prevailing trends of the total development than to the facts of the empirical world'.[14] It is the very *immediacy* of 'facts' which is the sign of their reification, and instead the tendency returns reality to its mediation, to the complex totality that can only be truly registered, and so given 'empirical' confirmation, from the standpoint of the proletariat. The method of the tendency is therefore constitutively ambiguous because, necessarily departing from the 'facts', it can only be successful if confirmed in and by revolutionary practice. Considering Karl Popper's well-known criticism of Marxism as always self-confirming, we could argue that the method of the tendency is actually closer to the model he proposed for science of bold conjectures that can be tested by possible refutation.

The method of the tendency can only be successful if confirmed in and by revolutionary practice

Of course my brief overview of the contemporary apocalyptic tone would suggest that Lukács is not at all the key reference point. If the current financial crisis has its roots in the breakdown of the Fordist compact in the 1970s and the switch to financialisation to deal with dropping corporate profits, then it may not be surprising to find that the contemporary apocalyptic tone is also rooted in that moment. These examples of contemporary post-autonomist thought all take off from the fusion of the work of Negri with that of Deleuze and Guattari. In particular they draw on Negri and Deleuze and Guattari's re-imagining of the concept of the tendency in the early 1970s. I am not suggesting a simple isomorphism between capitalist base and theoretical superstructure, after all this re-tooling of the tendency was precisely an attempt to articulate a theoretical means to grasp the precise effects of the economic 'base'. I am, however, suggesting that we do not simply regard theory as an hermetically sealed realm that has no relation to economic, political and social forms. In fact, as will become clear, this is a moment of theoretical reaction and response to the crisis of Fordism.

In the case of Negri, his canonical statement of the method of the tendency is given in his 1971 work 'Crisis of the Planner-State'. At this point Negri remains within remarkably classical and dialectical terms, arguing that '[t]he tendency gives us a determinate forecast, specified by the material dialectic that develops the factors comprising it.'[15] In a way remarkably similar to Lukács, Negri correlated the tendency with the viewpoint of the workers, and he also stressed that

> the procedure of the tendency is far from being rigid or deterministic. Instead, it represents an adventure of reason as it comes to encounter the complexities of reality, an adventure of reason that is *prepared to accept risks*: in fact, the truth of the tendency lies in its verification.[16]

As in Lukács the tendency is here deliberately pitched between the necessity of departing from the 'facts'; it is 'an adventure of reason', but also returning to a newly re-ordered world through the mechanism of revolutionary verification.

Negri's practising of this method in the 1970s was predicated on accepting and radicalising the crisis of the Fordist social compact to license a thinking of the imminent, and immanent, apocalypse, of capitalist relations. If capitalism started to rupture the structure of the factory and guaranteed employment then one should not regret this and go backwards to some lost world of social democracy, but push the tendency further into exodus, sabotage and destruction of the 'fetters' of the remnants of Fordism. The implication of his work, reflecting on the crisis of Fordism and its 'planner-state', was that communism had already arrived and would need to simply be realised. Negri was obviously 'prepared to accept risks', and the uncharitable could say that his own reading of the tendency fell victim to the *failure* of verification, with the defeat of the movement of autonomy and Negri's imprisonment. This failure did not, however, lead to a further nuancing of the method of the trajectory in his work. Rather, especially in *Empire* (2000), co-written with Michael Hardt, Negri would exchange the 'encounter with the complexities of reality' for an 'adventure of reason' in which the tendency was flattened further into the pure immanence and positivity of communism.

Accelerationism

The second element of the 'fusion', which would partly license Negri's later anti-dialectical 'positivisation' of the tendency, is derived from the work of Deleuze and Guattari. In their 1972 work *Anti-Oedipus,* they gave a different spin to the notion of the tendency as the means of liberation and rupture. In a by now well-known argument they indicated two fundamental tendencies of capitalism: a primary axiomatic of deterritorialisation or decoding (something like Karl Polanyi's 'disembedding'), and a secondary, but also essential, axiomatic of reterritorialisation, in which capitalism recoded and reabsorbed the desires it unleashed. They posed the question:

> But which is the revolutionary path? Is there one? – To withdraw from the world market, as Samir Amin advises Third World Countries to do, in a curious revival of the fascist 'economic solution'? Or might it be to go in the opposite direction? To go further still, that is, in the movement of the market, of decoding and deterritorialization? For perhaps the flows are not yet deterritorialized enough, not decoded enough, from the viewpoint of a theory and practice of a highly schizophrenic character. Not to withdraw from the process, but to go further, to 'accelerate the process,' as Nietzsche put it: in this matter, the truth is that we haven't seen anything yet.[17]

The tendency now becomes the immanent radicalisation of capital's own dynamic of deterritorialisation, a theoretical manoeuvre which I call 'accelerationism'.

Deleuze and Guattari were not the only practitioners of this form of the method of the tendency in the early to mid 1970s. In the wake of the failures of the movements of May '68 a number of French thinkers, particularly Jean-François Lyotard and Jean Baudrillard, also argued for a nihilist embrace of the disenchanting forces of capitalism as the means for achieving a strange kind of liberation through absolute immersion in the flows and fluxes of a libidinised capitalism. Lyotard couched accelerationism in its most extreme form in his 1974 work *Libidinal Economy*:

> the English unemployed did not have to become workers to survive, they – hang on tight and spit on me – *enjoyed* the hysterical, masochistic, whatever exhaustion it was of *hanging on* in the mines, in the foundries, in the factories, in hell, they enjoyed it, enjoyed the mad destruction of their organic body which was indeed imposed upon them, they enjoyed the decomposition of their personal identity, the identity that the peasant tradition had constructed for them, enjoyed the dissolutions of their families and villages, and enjoyed the new monstrous *anonymity* of the suburbs and the pubs in morning and evening.[18]

Truly we may not have seen anything like this before, and it is no surprise that this would prove a remarkably unpopular theoretical moment.

Of course Deleuze and Guattari did put the brakes on before conclusions like Lyotard's could be reached. They still held faith in an *anti*-capitalist project of liberation, but one that certainly courted confusion with a simple faith in capitalism to deliver the goods. Negri, on the other hand, fuses his work with that of Deleuze and Guattari by mapping this accelerationism together with the desire of workers to flee the Fordist compact. Rather than the valorisation of capitalism *per se*, as Deleuze and Guattari's model might seem to intimate, we have the valorisation of deterritorialisation (later often refigured in terms of 'exodus') as a proletarian strategy of resistance and rupture. In *Empire*, Hardt and Negri are critical of Deleuze and Guattari's model of 'continuous movement and absolute flows', regarding it as 'insubstantial and impotent'.[19] The difficulty is, however, that their solution to this problem is to *substantialise* the tendency. This is achieved by the ontologisation of the tendency in the immanent and positive power of the multitude. It appears, then, that the dispute is not so much that Deleuze and Guattari valorise flux or movement, but that they cannot *ground* that flux and movement in an absolute immanent power of collective potential communism. Once again the positive and accelerating tendency is that 'flux' that can override and dissolve reified reality.

The error of the apocalyptic tone is to presume the fusion of reason and reality too quickly

Deviations of the tendency

In a case of unlikely bedfellows, Alain Badiou, in his 1982 work *Theory of the Subject* (just translated into English by Bruno Bosteels), also makes recourse to the method of the tendency:

> To the logic of the trajectory, which the structural dialectic comes up against and which announces the new only in the retroactive operation of its *mise-en-scène*, we oppose the logic of tendencies, of currents, of vanguards, wherein that which is barely at its birth, though placed and subjected, links up with the most terrible force of the future.[20]

Badiou's presentation of a contrast between the 'logic of tendencies' to a quasi-structuralist 'logic of the trajectory' is cast in surprisingly Lukácsian terms – considering that they would usually be regarded as antithetical figures. Badiou's comment that in the logic of the trajectory '[t]ime is extinguished by space', could easily be mistaken for a quotation from Lukács.[21]

More relevantly to this discussion Badiou also identifies a second possible deviation of the method or logic of tendencies: this is committed by 'the dynamicists' who 'posit ... the multiplicity of variable intensities' and 'who believe in the insoluble tendency.'[22] These thinkers, and Badiou obviously has in mind Deleuze and Guattari, emphasise the *priority* of the flowing tendency over any objective moment. In Badiou's brilliant piece of diagnostics:

> [t]he asymptotic perspective of flight makes of the empiricist a wandering materialist, a vagabond philosopher of natural substances. Ignorance of the mirror turns the empiricist into the mirror of the world.[23]

Badiou's contention is that in their haste to depart from the 'static' or reified nature of capital's logic of economic and political places, the dynamicists, ironically, end up *reflecting* the accumulatory logic of capital.[24]

The importance of Badiou's analysis of the tendency is that he suggests the necessity for a careful *practice* of this method. What is particularly interesting is that Badiou does not simply suggest we condemn the errors of these deviations, but that the method of the tendency can only proceed by zig-zagging between these errors, which in this way correct each other. Those who emphasise a static logic of the trajectory and the necessity of patient analysis of the world as it is prevent us from rushing into revisions of our method that would leave it detached from reality. At the same time the dynamicists provide a necessary sense that we must take risks with the method and cannot simply follow the contours of reality. Although not consistently developed in his later work, Badiou's suggestion provides a useful means for 'balancing' between those sorts of pessimistic analyses which suggest an all-encompassing capitalism that always allocates people to their ideological place (as we find in certain moments in Althusser, Adorno and contemporary value-form theorists like Moishe Postone), and those 'optimistic' analyses that always stress 'resistance comes first' and the imminent arrival of a new era of flux and freedom (precisely Negri, Deleuze and Guattari and even certain moments in Jacques Rancière).

Considering Badiou's criticism of Deleuze and Guattari, and his suggestion that we practice a method of the tendency that does not embrace the perspective of 'flight', it comes as no surprise that he should later vehemently reject Negri's own variant of 'accelerationism':

> As is well known, for Negri, the Spinozist, there is only one historic substance, so that the capitalist empire is also the scene of an unprecedented communist deployment. This surely has the advantage of authorizing the belief that the worse it gets, the better it gets; or of getting you to (mis)take those demonstrations – fruitlessly convened to meet wherever the powerful re-unite – for the 'creation' and the 'multiform invention' of new petit-bourgeois proletarians.[25]

Badiou notes what we earlier gestured towards: the tendency is taken by Negri as the *immediate* fusion of reason and reality in one Spinozist 'historic substance'. What is lost is any nuancing of the tendency, any real sense of the tendency as riven by contradictions, tensions and reversals. The implication of such a reading of the tendency is that crisis is not to be reined in by the rationality of socialist or communist planning, but exacerbated by new forms of flight and flow – truly we have not seen anything yet.

Perhaps the best indication of the fatality of Negri's 'mirroring' of capital is his constant stress that the revolutionary movements of the 1960s and 1970s were *successful*. Negri argued that the recuperation of the revolutionary impulses of the 1970s was not a sign of defeat, but of actual communist success lurking beneath the rotted carapace of capital. One more effort and the fetters of capital would be shaken free, releasing the communist content within. This perpetual chant can crescendo at the onset of any crisis. Paolo Virno, in contrast, and rightly in my view, argued that the defeat of the revolutions of the 1960s and 1970s led to a 'communism of capital'; rather than a hyper-capitalism leading to communism, instead capitalism recuperated and redeployed communist elements (abolition of wage labour, extinction of the state and valorisation of the individual's uniqueness) for its own purposes.[26] Negri magically parlays defeat into victory.

Decelerationism

Of course the criticism that Negri's theorisation of the multitude is a 'mirror of capital' is not particularly original. My concern is not simply to point out the possible confusion of a supposedly communist apocalypse with an actually capitalist apocalypse. Instead, another, more important, irony is at work in this apocalyptic accelerationism. In a recent editorial for *New Left Review*, Gopal Balakrishnan raises again the more classical form of the tendency by returning to Marx's speculations about the tendential *limits* of capitalism. Deleuze and Guattari had argued that Marx's contention that '[t]he *real barrier* of capitalist production is *capital itself*' did not so much indicate that capitalism was doomed by its own limits of accumulation, but rather that this barrier should be smashed by the radicalisation of capitalism's deterritorialising tendencies.[27] Balakrishnan, instead, returns to the implied meaning of Marx's barrier metaphor that capitalism actually 'undermin[es] the original sources of all wealth'.[28] He notes that the 'acceleration' of capitalism since the 1970s, especially its technological developments of new cybernetic production forces, did not indicate some 'exhilarating new cultural condition' but rather '[c]apitalism's culture became an organized semblance of world-historic dynamism concealing and counteracting a secular deceleration in "the real economy".'[29]

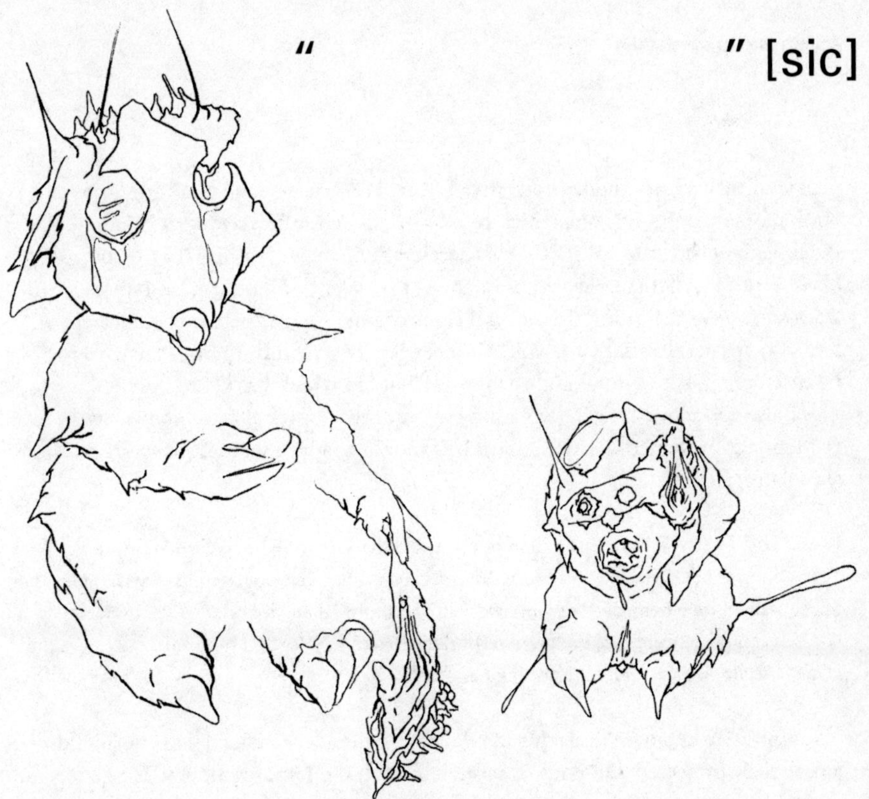

Accelerationism, as cultural and theoretical moment, is predicated on economic deceleration – there is a disjuncture, or even inversion, between the superstructure and the base. The 'mirror' of accelerationism is, as in Marx's famous metaphor of ideology as *camera obscura*, in fact an 'upside-down' image of 'historical life-processes.'[30] Although claiming to track the tendencies, the analyses of the accelerationists took appearance for reality, or to put it in more precise Marxist terms could only grasp the 'real abstractions' of the capitalist form of value. While these 'real abstractions' truly are real, they shape and determine the forms of value, they lack the dynamism that accelerationists detected, and which such forms had, of necessity, to project. This is what makes Deleuze and Guattari's analysis of capital as an axiomatic machine or virus of deterritorialisation at once so resonant and so problematic.

Balakrishnan's chosen example of the paradoxical effects that can result from such a cultural diagnosis is the work of Fredric Jameson on postmodernism, who was, of course, heavily influenced by accelerationist thinkers like Deleuze and Guattari and Baudrillard. Jameson too tried to connect economic shifts, into what he called 'late' or 'third stage' capitalism, with cultural shifts, the birth of postmodernism as a cultural dominant. Balakrishnan argues that Jameson's analysis was predicated on the 'immeasurable disproportion between human agency and newly unleashed cybernetic productive forces.'[31] What we might call the 'cyberpunk moment', and it is one which retains its belated followers today.[32] Jameson, Balakrishnan suggests, mitigated this accelerationism, with a shift 'to mapping an opaque, pseudo-dynamic world of financial markets.'[33] While Jameson made a cautious shift towards noting the cultural signs of impasse, the perennial apocalyptic attraction of accelerationism, which has persisted up to and through the current financial crisis, is a cultural and theoretical 'bubble' which has yet to burst.

Balakrishnan is amusingly scathing about the supposed technological and economic achievements which might be thought to give material substance to these speculative flights:

> the innovations of this period of capitalism have powered transformations in the *Lebenswelt* of diversion and sociability, an expansion of discount and luxury shopping, but above all a heroic age of what was until recently called 'financial technology'. Internet and mobile phones, Walmart and Prada, Black-Scholes and subprime – such are the technological landmarks of the period.[34]

Certainly Balakrishnan indicates the danger of a tendential accelerationism taking a particular projected tendency of capital, or even the fantasmatic self-image of capital, for its reality. It must be said, however, that accelerationism has been given a new lease of 'life' by recent developments in genetics and neuro-science. Fantasies of 're-sleeving' consciousness, or, as Lyotard speculated, of escaping a dying or doomed earth in a radically modified or downloaded post-human form, persistently haunt the Zeitgeist.

Balakrishnan's conclusion that 'we are entering into a period of inconclusive struggles between a weakened capitalism and dispersed agencies of opposition, within delegitimated and insolvent political orders' is a plausible diagnosis of the near future, even if only time will tell whether his claim that the capitalist renewal of a new expanding cycle of accumulation will fail is true.[35] The cultural and theoretical apocalyptic tone is highly resistant to the kind of diagnosis Balakrishnan makes of capitalism as tending towards a 'stationary state'. To adapt T. S. Eliot, the apocalyptic tone can only imagine the end of the world in the form of a 'bang', and never a 'whimper'. While I am not suggesting the complacency of simply denying out of hand any possibility of apocalypse, which seems most likely at the moment to come

capital has responded as it knows best: by redoubling abstractions

in an ecological form, the apocalyptic tone I have been tracing is one which actually *welcomes* apocalypse as the decisive moment, the moment of the 'lifting of the veil' (the Greek meaning of the word 'apocalypse'). More particularly I am suggesting that the cycle of this tone, especially its accelerationism, is closely imbricated with the shift to a neoliberal financial and political regime and its crisis. Of course it was an attempt to grasp and resist that order, whatever we think of what I regard as its failings. The difficulty I am pointing to is that it *mistook* the tendency of that order, taking a 'real appearance' for reality and missing the structural and economic limits of that order.

Bursting the theoretical bubble

The method of the tendency is, precisely, a method that does not offer guarantees, except in the form of future verification or confirmation. The apocalyptic tone of accelerationism is, quite unusually, predicated in a firm and traditional Marxist belief that reality was on our side and that reason and reality were fused. I say unusual because more commonly radical thought in the last century saw a detachment between reason and reality, not such a surprising conclusion in light of the events of the 'age of extremes'. Perhaps, in the wake of the events of the '60s, as Herbert Marcuse suggested, the hope that reason and reality could be re-aligned once again was on the agenda. The error of the apocalyptic tone is to presume the fusion *too quickly* – that the tendency will deliver on its own, or, in Badiou's words, that there is 'one historic substance' (it could be contrasted, as a symmetrical error, with those forms of 'negative dialectics' which seem to presume no possible integration of reason with reality). Thus 'accelerationism' takes capitalism at its word, reading capitalism's promise of endless accelerating productivity as a given actuality.

I am not, as seems to be the case in some currents of ecological thought, arguing for a return to the detachment of reason and reality. In this case pessimism licenses retreat, with reason reduced to ever diminishing pockets or niches of resistance – often art, the body, or a certain elect. Instead, as should be evident, I argue that we return to a more nuanced realism about the contemporary conjuncture, and a closer analysis of its possibilities and limits. In his closing address to the *Historical Materialism* conference in London, 2009, Fredric Jameson argued that the aim of critical intellectuals should be to present or represent the contradictions of the time, even to sharpen them. Although a seemingly modest proposal, I am suggesting that this is in fact a necessary and radical process of re-ordering and, even, cultural struggle.

With the bursting of the financial bubble and resulting economic crisis we could argue that a gap, perhaps only temporary, has opened up globally in our perception of the real abstractions of capitalism. If not exactly the fabled moment of the Emperor's New Clothes, at least capitalism's jingoism, and the thinness or weakness of its claims to constitute an order of development, freedom and liberation, ring hollow. Of course, into that gap, capital has responded as it knows best: by redoubling abstractions, in creating what Alain Badiou has called the spectacle of the 'crisis-film', in which the financial crisis becomes another apocalyptic film to elicit our awe and terror.[36] Perhaps, however, at this moment of the opening of the gap we could also burst the theoretical bubble of accelerationism. We could renew our theoretical analysis by practising a method of the tendency that more closely aligns base and superstructure in our analysis, that permits a closer grasp of the failures, tensions and contradictions of this order, and that may condition the possibility of a true fusion of reason and reality in practice.

Footnotes

1 This work is based on a presentation made at Another World is Necessary: Crisis, Struggle and Political Alternatives, Historical Materialism Sixth Annual Conference, 27-29 November 2009. I would like to thank my co-panellists, Evan Calder Williams and Mark Fisher and the audience, for their comments and criticisms. I would also like to thank Benedict Seymour for the invitation to develop the presentation into this essay.

2 See Not Bored!'s discussion of the Situationists détournement of Cohn, 'Norman Cohn's The Pursuit of the Millennium', http://www.notbored.org/cohn.html and also the Italian radical authorial collective Luther Blisset's novel *Q*, London: Arrow, 2004, which reimagines the Anabaptists of the Peasant War through the lens of 1970s Italian autonomist radicalism.

3 Derrida offers the best analysis of this 'tone' in his essay 'Of an Apocalyptic Tone Recently Adopted in Philosophy', trans. John P. Leavey Jr., *Oxford Literary Review*, 1984, vol. 6, #2, pp 3-37.

4 Alberto Toscano's *Fanaticism*, London and New York: Verso, 2009, develops a thorough analysis of the uses and abuses of the idea of the fanatic, taking in both Cohn and Kant, to which I am heavily indebted.

5 Karl Marx and Friedrich Engels, *Manifesto of the Communist Party*, 1848, Chapter One 'Bourgeois and Proletarians', The Marxists Internet Archive, 2004, http://www.marxists.org/archive/marx/works/1848/communist-manifesto/ch01.htm#007

6 Franco 'Bifo' Berardi, 'Communism is back but we should call it the therapy of singularisation', *Generation Online*, 2009, http://www.generation-online.org/p/fp_bifo6.htm; Angela Mitropolous and Melinda Cooper, 'In Praise of Ursura', *Mute*, Autumn 2009, vol. 2, #13, p.107, http://www.metamute.org/content/in_praise_of_usura; Antonio Negri, 'No New Deal is possible', trans. Arianna Bove, *Radical Philosophy* May/June 2009, no. 155, http://www.radicalphilosophy.com/default.asp?channel_id=2187&editorial_id=27980

7 Karl Marx, 'Preface' to 'A Contribution to the Critique of Political Economy', 1859, Marxists Internet Archive, 1999, http://www.marxists.org/archive/marx/works/1859/critique-pol-economy/preface.htm.

8 Ibid.

9 Gopal Balakrishnan, 'On the Stationary State', *New Left Review*, September / October 2009, #59, p.7, n2, http://www.newleftreview.org/?view=2799

10 Georg Lukács, *History and Class Consciousness*, trans. Rodney Livingstone, London: Merlin Press,

1971, p.181.

11 Ibid. Emphasis in original.

12 Ibid., p.180

13 Ibid.

14 Ibid., p.183.

15 Antonio Negri, *Books for Burning: Between Civil War and Democracy in 1970s Italy*, ed. Timothy S. Murphy, trans. Arianna Bove, Ed Emery, Timothy S. Murphy and Francesca Novello, London and New York: Verso, 2005, p.27.

16 Ibid., my italics.

17 Gilles Deleuze and Félix Guattari, *Anti-Oedipus*, trans. Robert Hurley, Mark Seem and Helen R. Lane, Minneapolis: University of Minnesota Press, 1983, pp.239-240.

18 Jean-François Lyotard, *Libidinal Economy*, trans. Iain Hamilton Grant, London: Athlone, 1993, p.214.

19 Michael Hardt and Antonio Negri, *Empire*, Cambridge, MA: Harvard University Press, 2000, p.28.

20 Alain Badiou, *Theory of the Subject*, trans. and intro. Bruno Bosteels, London and New York: Continuum, 2009, p.109, my italics.

21 Ibid., p.108.

22 Ibid., p.209.

23 Ibid.

24 In one of those ironies of history this charge had been made earlier by Jean Baudrillard in his 1977 work *Forget Foucault*, (trans. Nicole Dufresne, New York: Semiotext(e), 1987), where he argued that the 'compulsion toward liquidity, flow, and an accelerated circulation' in Deleuzo-Guattarian models of desire is only the replica or mirror of capitalist circulation (p.25). Of course this analysis was vitiated by Baudrillard's own 'negative' accelerationism, in which the capitalist system produces its own moment of crisis and reversal, or 'implosion', through the acceleration of its own tendencies to commodify all reality into the hyperreality of simulacra.

25 Alain Badiou, *Polemics*, trans. and intro. Steve Corcoran, London and New York: Verso, 2006, p.45.

26 Paolo Virno, *A Grammar of the Multitude: For an Analysis of Contemporary Forms of Life*, trans. Isabella Bertolleti, James Cascaito and Andrea Casson, foreword by Sylvère Lotringer, Los Angeles and New York: Semiotext(e), 2005, pp.110-111.

27 Karl Marx, *Capital vol. 3*, Harmondsworth: Penguin, 1981, p.358.

28 Balakrishnan, op. cit., p.7 n2.

29 Ibid., p.15.

30 Karl Marx, *The German Ideology*, 1845, Marxists Internet Archive, http://www.marxists.org/archive/marx/works/1845/german-ideology/ch01a.htm

31 Balakrishnan, op. cit., pp.14-15.

32 A key example would be Alexander R. Galloway and Eugene Thacker's *The Exploit: A Theory of Networks*, Minneapolis and London: University of Minnesota Press, 2007, which retains a Deleuze and Guattari / Negri accelerationist model of rupturing with the 'protocols' of control systems through overload, excess and 'viral' apocalypse.

33 Balakrishnan, op. cit., p.15.

34 Ibid., p.16.

35 Ibid., p.26.

36 Alain Badiou, 'Of Which Real is this Crisis a Spectacle?', trans. Nina Power and Alberto Toscano, Infinite Thought, 18 October 2008, http://www.cinestatic.com/infinitethought/2008/10/badiou-on-financial-crisis.asp

Benjamin Noys <b.noys@chi.ac.uk> is a theorist living in Bognor Regis. His most recent book is *The Persistence of the Negative: A Critique of Contemporary Continental Theory,* forthcoming in September 2010 with Edinburgh University Press. His blog is http://leniency.blogspot.com

Where 'fixing' the future is a game for social engineers, writers Matthew Fuller and Anthony Iles prefer to open out the present, egg on its energies, taunt immanence...

Images by Caroline Heron, http://carolineheron.com

POST-CRUNCH FUTURES II: A MUTE FICTION SPECIAL

POST-CRUNCH FUTURES II

HELP AND ADVICE

by Matthew Fuller

The King of Decisions gathers heads of sections from other wings of the department for a get-together, no compulsory results, just an exchange of ideas. Junior Deciders are brought in to fatten the ranks, practice deference and to populate the air with ideas which are then cut to size by the old hands who snip here and there, push word blancmange at each other and incorporate anything that might come out into their own systems of advanced apprehension. There is an advance ingestion of poison, strengths weaknesses opportunities threats all lined up for subsumption. Tailored and surgeoned for viewing, suit, as one at the table admiringly notes, 'like an African dictator', a cultural citation in tune with global decentering, he grips his head, fingers running through abundant transplant coiff, and utters a citation from an orator become bullet-point action figure, prefiguring the ground, linking it across to a vocabulary he imagines he once read up on via a half-forgotten summary extracted from a reader whose work was derailed for a month in its compiling and then let go, the allusion to which offers the chance to figure the freeing up of working time in the Department, the cross referencing of tasks via time-allocation, throughput equalisation via short, median and long-term time slices measured against sectional infill paradigms, local modelisations of the form, its various subsections and the hierarchy of form users in distinct soon to be partially, where appropriate, horizontalled practices which, whilst not unlike guilds, are built on the basis of meaningful professional differentiation of roles, nevertheless, the very recognition of which difference allows for a fine-tuning of role representation and cross-referencing of action duplication by operatives lower down in the organisational chain, the freeing up of high-value time resulting from which will regularise workflow on the infill from point of entry into the department through to all levels of handling and throughput, at the very least allowing the thousands of separate questions, fields, infill procedures, data-procuration devices, reader modes, sequence completion parameters and time-allocation metrics and action structures, scripting, assessment and meta-frameworks to come into some kind of de-local co-comparison matrix, saving space in memory, but also allowing for more meaningful narratives of work to be experienced as a creative flow of availability-apportioned assessment process with all the kinds of quality and economic invention

A disaster opens up the possibilities for human society to regrow in new, even worse ways

of possibility that that implies. The KoD listens mouth puckered half open whilst his peers nod ritual combat-assent, and one of whom responds from memory systematising his words entirely in relation to the continuity of European culture from an area around the Mediterranean, the basis for which all database and infill culture and social process must draw from if it is to maintain stability and close relevance to a chain of popular memos he has authored. This is a move of incorporation which thrills participants in its capacity for swallowing. All of those present above a certain rank know that nothing of what occurs in this room has any effect, there is no way for one of the trainee deciders to break into the rank that is hungered after through the brilliant formulation of a new mechanism, queue-sort or tweak to a cellular process in memory. Once a vocab has been stabilised a report, a proposal, a white paper will be mooted amongst select holding positions. A proto-restructuring will be advanced, tested out in a quiet patch of the department. It'll settle in, take hold, then be superceded and remain as a ghost structure amongst a diaspora of users, machines and memory units strung out across a batch of process-domains and handling systems, achieving longevity, unless that is, it becomes a success. Then all bets are off.

That evening I'm sending to a supplementary relationship service but using it as my primary for reasons of cost and aptitude. It's very effective. I'm all romantic and flowered, eager, in return I get a variable interval reinforcement schedule with more emphasis on the training than the reward but delivered with a human touch and the promise of more. I interrupt every other process, eating, washing, watching, to check for any response, any updates in my attention allocation, but since what seemed a rapid burst a day ago I've been dropped into a passionate grade wait and salivate mode. This is certainly enough to keep my attention on track. Whilst waiting for some contact, I'm fed a trickle of watching and purchasing opportunities, checking and filling, read and respond, eyes tracked by vectors and keywords, the potential of contacts. As I'm twitching synapses with this stuff, a slow stream of symbols mutters along the bottom of the screen. The form now has a phone keypad based entry system to supplement its more verbose form. A series of data entry opportunities, confirmation and checking points and tree-form responses by a voice which includes OK in every statement-trigger action. Because the form remains as yet incompletable this facility is only available to the early stage infillers. Nevertheless it allows some remarkable insights into the workings of the data acquisition process. The ticker shows live entry sequences, one layer of characters as they appear as entered in response to the prompts and questions, another including the sequence of characters entered also to navigate, to confirm or to cancel data entry. The department is feeding this data to selected Readers for ambient processing. We are to use crowd mind to intuitively sort potential infill stage completion candidates using peripheral visual processing in off-hours relaxation time, harnessing the power of the relaxed mind to spot exemplary patterns in one-dimensional strings of characters. In order to aid Readers to be spontaneous with their contributions to the extraction of cognitive value from the feed an animated character spots funny words that might appear, links to sources for definitions of non-English type character strings and annotates the amount of time since the last user recognition contribution. It's important that we watch and process this stuff because fresh living memory is not allocated to this kind of feed, so all data comes in live and evaporates if not spotted, whilst this means days of infill may be unreplicable if not checked, the sheer flow of

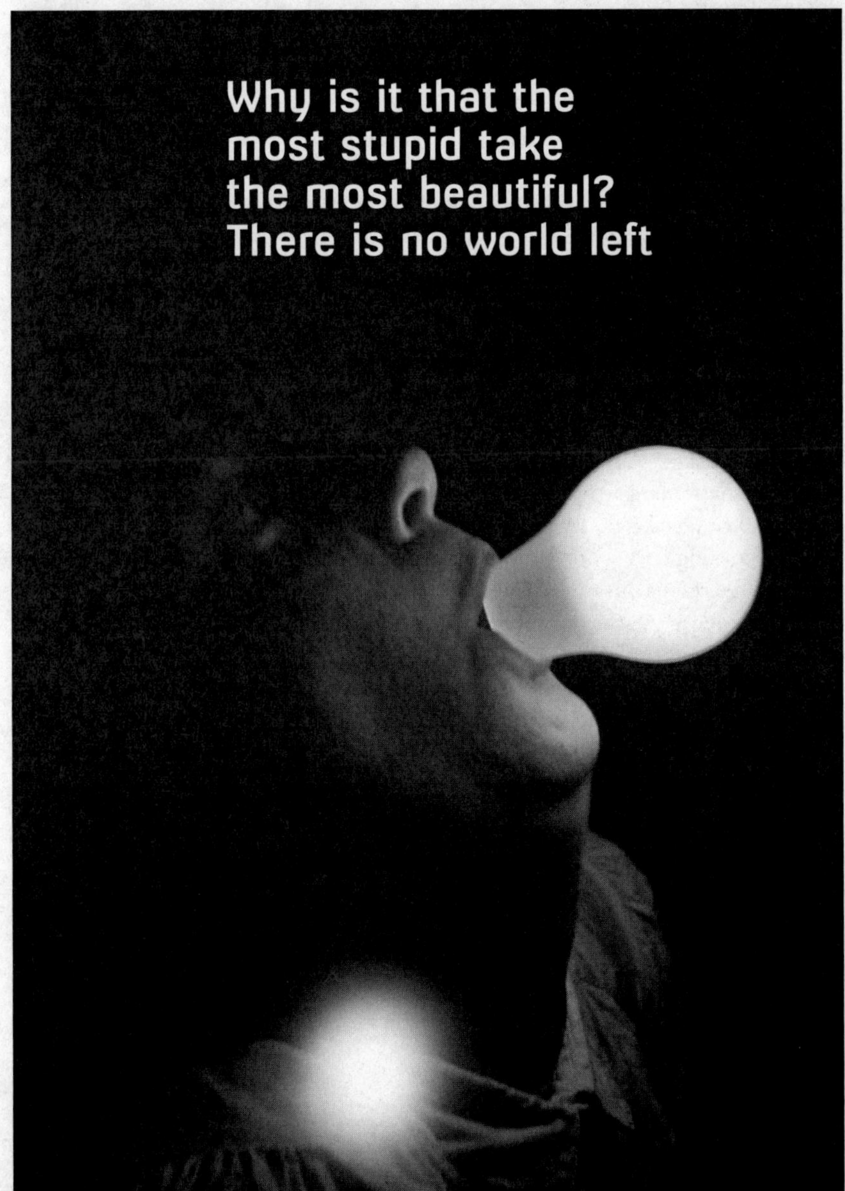
Why is it that the
most stupid take
the most beautiful?
There is no world left

data acts as a stimulus to blocked creativity within the Readership, setting free the imagination. Night continues in a haze of numbers and visualisations.

In the morning, news filters announce the removal of a layer of scaffolding over the renewed Elephant. A new era of openness ushers in sunlight and job opportunities, unified signage. Away with mildew and rot. Daylight conveyed inwards by belts of mirrors on servo-motors tracking the sun, shoppers and workers are to be upgraded from being sad specks on the surface of the great red earth, the sun will revolve around them, individually, hot and luscious, hot fat, 50%, visa, clearance, money transfer, money clearance, supreme conditioning, business advice, plantain and potatoes, factory shop, cooled by a compressed cube of whey covered in thin chocolate in a silver blue plastic wrapper, pitched by the boxload into a freezer ditched and resold bearing the brand of another make but plugged in and selling cold fat, delicious, second floor, milks, meats, sugars, books, secondary processing of primal stuff, working the margins, eat the cheery.

For fortune telling, walk with a lightbulb in your mouth, become saturated in colour, don't gag. There are so many shades between grey and yellow, dilate your eyes up. Air conditioning without the inconvenience of air. Don't eat your tongue, don't choke, keep your lips still whilst reading, breathe in through the nose and out through the mouth. Keep your tongue on the electrodes. If the bulb lights up you have met the love of your life. Bite hard. Preserve a margin of indifference. Taste glass. You crunchy. Hot! Read your fortune in reverse by choosing one of the following boxes: Extremely satisfied. Very satisfied. Fairly satisfied. Neither / nor. Fairly dissatisfied. Very dissatisfied. Extremely dissatisfied. Thank you for taking the time. The pattern made by the relations between movements of broken clumps of moss and condensed mulch air-grime as they slide down the tilted surface of a glass covered awning during one hour of seasonally average rainfall are of equal or higher value to the results of your entry. No further correspondence will be entered. You Hot! Very warm weather makes for a disaster. A disaster opens up the possibilities for human society to regrow in new, even worse ways. Everyone is hungry for it, to find the monster they turn into. Everyone will be happy and live in peace when they unleash their inner homicidal maniac and sexy. This is hot and tasty. I want to be a sociologist when it happens. Please do play with the nouns at your own risk. In the perpetual orange twilight, guards check the doors, arm alarms, shake handles, pull chain, slide bolts, swipe sensors, flick switches, scan barcodes and click stubs, roll shutters, scan screens, turn joysticks to steer cameras, defer time, stretch it, every object evaporates, hot or cold, fast or slow, lockdown, atom by atom: fill your pockets to the limit of what is perceptible to the casual observer.

Flowers appear attached to some railings by the station. Each bunch of flowers is surrounded by cellophane, some with ribbon and small notes, some photographs, tied on quickly with wire, tape or string.

Daffodils: I miss you you stupid fucker taken away from us and promise that whoever did this to you will also fucking die.

White roses: Because they are shit-scared. They eat what they leave. They will need eyes in their arses, backstabbers. Drink up.

Yellow carnations: A convoy of lorries with big PAs, generators and brew and spliff will take us to heaven and then everything will start new. I will never forget you. Justice will be done.

Pink carnations: Only money can save us. We're skint. You will be missed.

Green chrysanthemums and red tulips: Your daughters will be looked after by people who love them. You are in heaven. Don't forget us down here in hell.

Fresias: You still owe me fifty quid. I love you.

Lilies: How could you be taken away from us like this? I can't believe that you are not still walking these streets, but with a gun this time. Come back and start it off.

Red carnations: We're coming, hold on tight, it won't be long!

Yellow tulips: Total desperation, the most desperation that is possible.

Purple tulips: Why is it that the most stupid take the most beautiful? There is no world left.

Daffodils: Angel, send some lightning down to finish us off.

Yellow chrysanthemums and tiger lilies: This is not over yet. This town.

Red roses and white spray: What did this to you is an uncontrollable chain reaction of stupidity between people who have no means of looking ahead other than with the antennae locked onto their heads by Babylon.

Pink and white chrysanthemums: No war but the class war. No dogs except guide dogs. The health of the people is the highest law.

Daffodils: You changed my life, now you're going to suffer bad.

Tiger lilies: There is Sky up there in heaven I know.

Pink and red tulips: If I didn't have broken legs I'd run after them. If I didn't have metal arms, I'd strangle them. If I didn't have glass eyes and black shades I'd look them in the eye and tell them. I still have a mouth and some good working intestines left. That's the way it's going to happen.

Red roses: You were a lion on the streets of London Zoo.

Daffodils: Panic.

Daffodils: Extraordinary Measures.

Tulips: Don't think about it. Don't go back. Keep going.

Matthew Fuller <m.fuller@gold.ac.uk> is aggregated at http://spc.org/fuller/. *Elephant & Castle,* from which this is excerpted, will be published by Autonomedia later this year

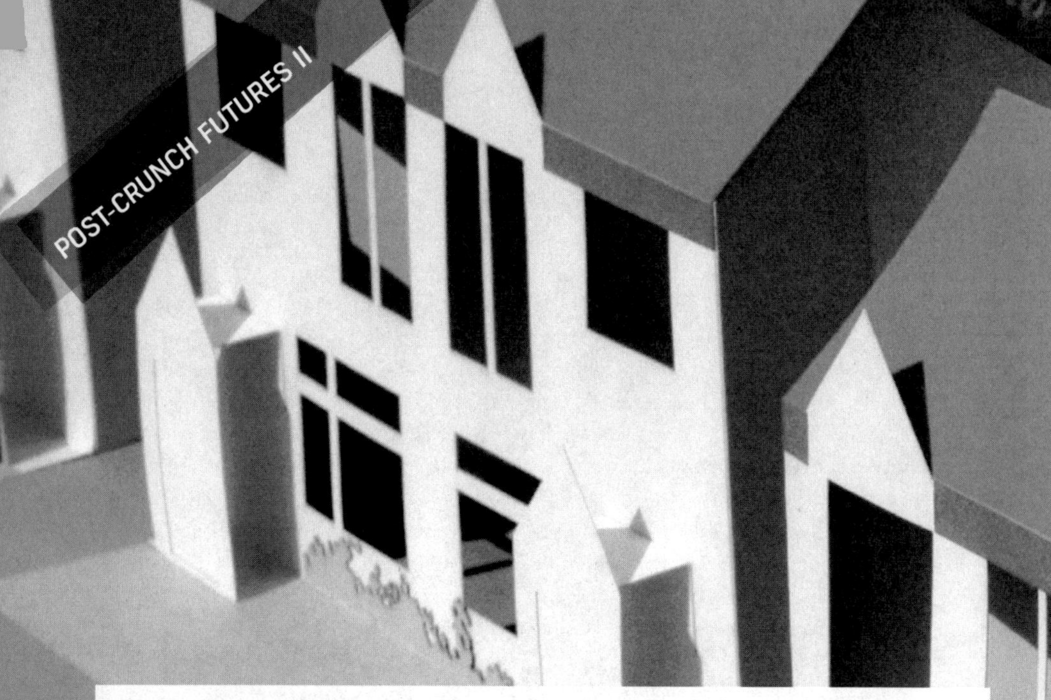

SPECULATING ON HOUSING

by Anthony Iles

Gav, Penny, Ayanna and Rag are in the Palm Tree, a pub in Mile End park, East London. The Palm Tree is the last in a row of buildings to survive aerial bombing of the area in World War II.

Gav: The Egg is a phantom organisation... It's an idea, it's not something you can join.

Penny: But what's the point of a group you can't join. What does it do? What does it have to do with us and our work?

Gav: The Egg has nothing to do with work! If anything it undoes any compulsion to do.

Ayanna: Sounds just elitist nonsense to me. Where's your head at these days Gav? I mean where have you been – you've not been attending any meetings, No Borders, the G20 organising meetings. I mean fuck, you didn't even come to the G20 at all. Where's your commitment Gav?

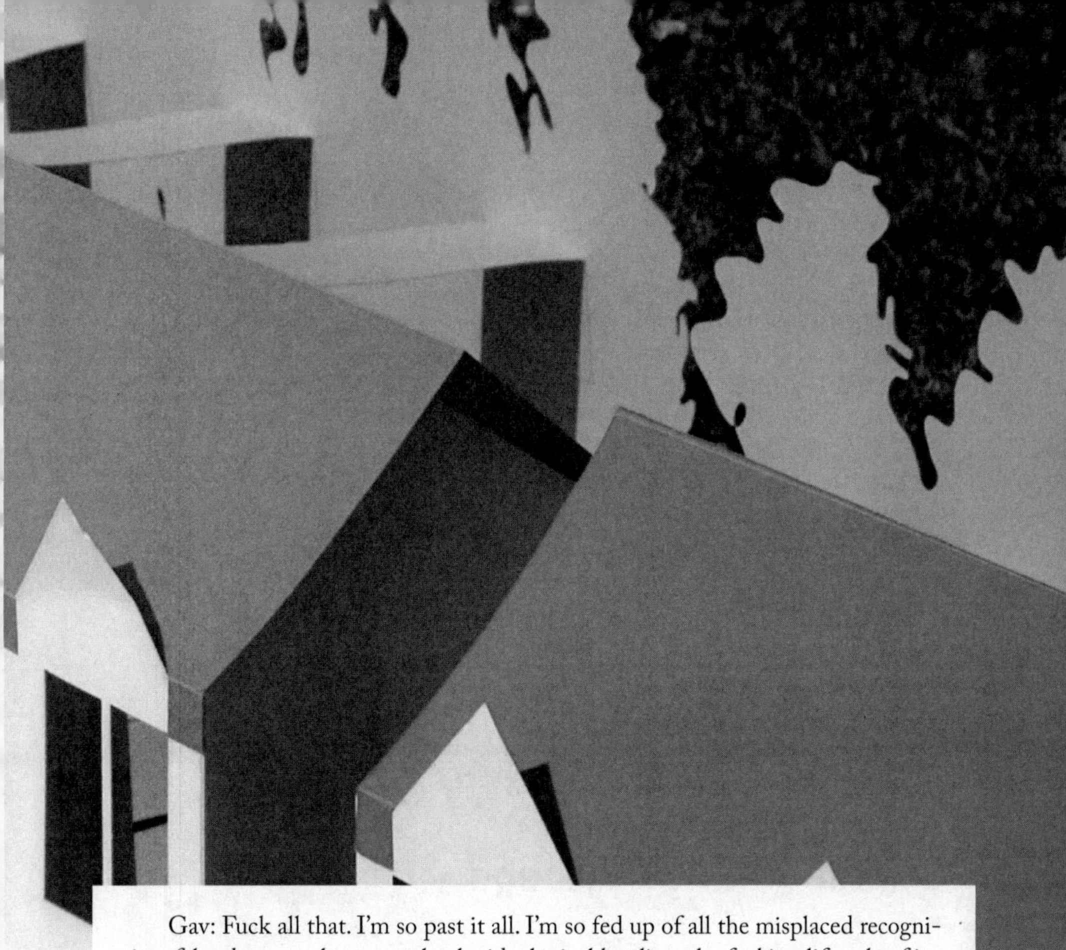

Gav: Fuck all that. I'm so past it all. I'm so fed up of all the misplaced recognition, false dueness, the spectacle, the ideological kettling, the fucking lifestyle of it all, the reformism, the lazy thinking...

Penny: I get it, you've invented a phantom organisation so that you can play chief, so that you don't have to put up with people's stupid opinions! You're a fucking wanker Gav.

Gav: Fuck it, fuck it, I knew I shouldn't have told you about it. I knew you lot wouldn't understand.

Silence for a few minutes as Gavin, (hurt), stands nursing his beer.

Gav: Listen guys. I'm sorry. I really want you to understand this idea and get behind it. I'll try to explain. The Egg is an idea, but it's also more than that. The Egg acts upon what isn't acted upon, what is ignored in the activist scene, in politics. We have this problem in the scene that our politics are reactive, our actions defensive – against new laws, against police repression and so on. The Egg is about exacerbating the contradictions and conflicts. It's about...

Penny: This just sounds like Class War redux...

Ayanna: Nah, Penny... Let him speak. Go on Gav, I wanna hear this.

Gav: It's about seizing upon this crisis, deepening it, making it pregnant with change. The Egg doesn't recruit and it isn't clandestine either. The Egg is present as potentiality – but it never gets actualised. The Egg is real, in many ways it's more real than the IWW or the GMB, some activist campaign or whatever.

Rag: Are we gonna bomb shit? Totally fuck the system?

Gav: (laughing) Shut up Rag. I'm serious. The Egg is a proposition, it's a structure for thinking some things through, a carrier or vehicle if you like, but I've got other ideas too... Let's go outside.

The crew heads out into the garden. Gav gestures towards the huge blocks of nearly finished luxury flats on the other side of the canal. The group sits down on the grass opposite one of the blocks of flats.

'Fucking cunt stables,' Rag offers nonchalantly. 'Oi!' parries Ayanna, leaning across Penny to deal Rag a hearty slap to the side of the head. Settling back down, the group discusses the state of struggle after the crisis – trying to think through some of the campaigns they have been involved in; occupations, community campaigns to save Queen St. Market, Defend Council Housing and so on. What exactly had the crisis changed? Penny talks about being glad about the crisis bringing everything into the open, 'I always wore my crisis on the inside, tucked in so to speak...'. Ayanna broaches the reformist nature of their campaigns. She suggests that even within limits, it's always good to get involved and she likes the personal side – what she calls 'meeting real people'. Gav agrees, the necessity of acting in real situations with all their contradictions, but mutters cynically about 'real people'. 'I mean what the fuck is a real person anyway! I don't know if I want to be one!'

The Egg is a proposition, it's a structure for thinking things through

The reason Gav has led them there, before the flats, becomes clear. He has a plan, some sort of intention with regards to this almost completed block – Penny second guesses him: 'You wanna squat them?' she shouts, jumping up and rubbing her hands with excitement. 'Bagsy the penthouse!'

A week later three figures huddle by behind a JCB, the grotesque silhouettes of hastily built apartments loom above them.

The crew have been hiding out for hours, watching security shifts to change so they can record the hours the guards rotate. They're on a mission together, Ayanna, Gav and Rag, but Ayanna has a second mission. She wanted to puncture the separation between the conversations leading up to the action and the practical task of getting in the building. Now was not the time, and thus exactly the inappropriate time to bring up some difficult thoughts. She'd brought her notebook and wound up the other two bombarding them with quotes from Mario Mieli's 'Gay Communism':

'Gav, read this: "The object of the revolutionary struggle of homosexuals is not that of winning social tolerance for gays, but rather the liberation of the homoerotic desire in every human being." That means... Rather than you two having some liberal responsibility to tolerate me and my "perversions"... It's actually the other way round. I, through the practice of my desire, liberate you!'

Gav raises his hands to his head. Rag: 'Thanks Ayanna! So I can just carry on as before shaking hands with the unemployed and you'll do the liberation bit! Cheers! Thanks a lot... Now that's liberation baby.'

'Quiet'. The group held still for a moment. They stared at each other beaming, enjoying the power over themselves that it took to hold in the bubbling laughter and maintain calm. When the stillness seemed to have overtaken their bodies again Ayanna continued to unravel her notes and fill the other two in on how 'Towards a Gay Communism' went to work on groups. Gav waited patiently before responding, 'Obviously there's a...' 'Wait!' Ayanna interrupted, 'NOTHING IS EVER FUCKING OBVIOUS!'

Silence. And they all breathe in again. Gav says: 'delete that word.' He breathes deeply, before stuttering. 'Th-th-there's a strong tradition of communists who became disaffected with groups and turned themselves to the task of internal critique. Jacques Camatte, Sam Moss, Debord even... You get this from anti-psychiatry too. Gangs, council communism, the working class, schizophrenia – each provided the *promesse du bonheur*, the sacred or profane form. The question of organisation is ultimately not resolvable, but it could be that the destruction wrought by internal critique is productive. Prompting splits, an endless secession rather than endless revolution. Though we are constantly being duped into believing in, and identifying with images of individuals which are not ourselves – we are duped into thingness, yet the revolutionary organisation does not provide an answer in the dissolution in the crowd, the singular identification does not speak poverty to the richness of myriad possible alternative attachments...'

'There he is. Duck!' Rag whispers as Gav's short sermon trails off.

They would wait another hour in silence before speaking again. After this intermission they go to work. Rag takes control. He leads them along an unfinished ditch at the side of the building, tightly following a smoothly curving cast concrete wall to the back of the building away from the canal and the bright lights. Along the way they check entrances, door sizes, locks and windows. At the far southern corner of the building next to an unfinished pit with a drain at its base they find a door ajar and slip inside.

The following night Gav and Rag are sitting in an Irish pub in Stoke Newington, the kind of place where everyone looks conspiratorial. Rag's relating his experiences with sound systems he used to run with in the 1990s, Desert Storm and Exodus. 'There were plenty of conversations during quiet times, but when we had stuff to do we didn't really think about it all that much, it was always just a question of where, when and how to get in. Brute force and a bit of canny timing usually did the trick.'

Gav wants to know how they're going to defend the building once they've got in. They've enough people to get in and they know the entrances they're going to use, how to get the security off their backs for enough time to seal the place... Gav stands up, 'I've got it. We use a flash mob. I'll call a flash mob outside the Comedy Café across the road – 400 people dressed as clowns miming the words to the Beatles "Hard Day's Night" should provide enough of a distraction to get in. After we're in we'll send down a crew to bring the clowns in and party. At noon a massive banner drop off the top of the building. On the banner: "Here we make ourselves anew – Free Housing for All!"'

'Great,' Rag mumbles 'but still way too Leninist for me'. He strolls off to the bar. Gav calls him a 'cunt' under his breath. Presage the first split.

End of the night. Gav and Rag are standing waiting for buses going in opposite directions.

'After a step forward comes a split,' Rag says, and turning seeing his bus rolling up the road, 'good to start with a split then. I'm off... you know everything about how to get into the building now, but I'm not down with your plan. I got my own. I'm going to approach it from another direction. I'll be in touch.'

Rag doesn't go far, but as far as the others are concerned he's gone for good, he breaks off all contact. He scopes out another building further up the canal, The Pinnacles. The building is finished, but the garden, car park and reception have not yet been completed and it looks like work has been abandoned long ago. None of the retail units around the base of the building are occupied. Rag counts a total of 11 flats out of 90 flats occupied.

The next day he calls the company who manages security for the building. He calls the developers themselves, then the agents who manage the building for the developers. To each he puts a simple proposition, that he occupy a few flats in their building, decorating each one and giving the impression they are inhabited. From the agents he gets an appointment to meet one of them on site the following Tuesday.

Initially it's just Rag, but before long he persuades others. Rag gets his mate Azurre – an out of work architect – a job on the front desk. He notices a shortfall in the cleaning services and manages to persuade the agents to take on an Ecuadoran cleaner – someone he met at his weekly adult education classes. In exchange for a small broom cupboard and less than minimum wage, Adolfo sweeps the corridors, landings and stairwells of The Pinnacles. He's surly and uncommunicative, barely exchanging a syllable with any of the other staff or residents, but when he and Rag are in private he opens up about his past in Ecuador and isolated present in London.

Officially Adolfo's staying in the broom cupboard where the cleaning products are kept, but since Rag's responsible for three flats and, by the second month, he's managed to purloin the keys to a further 10 vacants, Adolfo has his pick of places to crash in, listen to the radio and read. By the end of the second month he begins to make a garden in one of the three flats Rag is charged with making look inhabited. He fills the bath with soil purloined bag by bag from nearby building sites. Ferns and horsetails spill out of the bathroom and form a leafy curtain across the entrance hall.

I, through the practice of my desire, liberate you!

In the coming months Adolfo will turn the flat into a rainforest – an uncommon meeting of species – blackberry plants brought from Lidl as well as seeds and fungus he's received in well-padded envelopes from relatives. A reddish algae, found only in Ecuador, stains the glass plates surrounding the balconies. One day Rag notices a small plaque on the inside of the door, 'Jardim Botanico Entropico' he reads. Sweet.

Rag and Adolfo are sitting on the decking over the canal opposite the Palm Tree pub watching the sun go down. This is their end of the day ritual and it usually passes in silence except on Sundays when an elderly gentleman in a motorised wheelchair rocks up and sees out the sunset booming music from the back of his vehicle. To Rag's surprise, Adolfo opens the conversation. 'I'm thinking about my garden... I'm always thinking about my garden these days. Whilst I'm looking at the pub and thinking I should have a palm tree in my garden, I'm also thinking of another garden.' Rag has learnt the art of pause hanging around this surly cleaner-gardener. He waits quite a while, until a swan below them has slowly floated by and the air has cooled slightly, before asking, 'And which garden would that be? Is there another garden in the world as beautiful as this one?'

Adolfo tells him about the other garden, the one he is thinking of, the one Pizarro's conquistadors found in a temple in Tumbes in the territory now called Colombia. 'This garden was made from silver and gold, mined by the sweat of the natives and fashioned into flowers and plants by the temples' finest craftsmen.'

'What happened to it?' Rag asked hastily, despite having already guessed the answer. Adolfo looks up at him with a look of mock surprise, 'The Spaniards melted it down and transported it across the ocean. Of course, with everything else.' Adolfo goes on, Rag is amazed to hear more words spring from his mouth in one evening than in the sum of their conversations over the last months, 'My garden is dedicated to the memory of that garden at Tumbes, but my garden works in the opposite direction. It does not spring from labour, but from entropy. It does not dissolve into value.. It poisons value and destroys it, it is particular and never equivalent to nothing... never.'

'After a step forward comes a split,' Rag says, turning and seeing his bus rolling up the road

With Azurre taking care of things front of house, Rag retreats to one of the more isolated flats at the back of the building. With no canalside view and overlooking the unfinished gardens full of bags of cement these were the cheapest and least desirable. Rag's got plenty of space to make as much noise as he pleases, undisturbed. He's planning to go to work on something that's been a long time percolating. On the far wall of the apartment lean nine full-length mirrors collected from nearby empty flats. To its right Rag has plastered the wall with fragments of broken glass and mirrors he's found in skips and on other sites. In amidst the broken glass wall are bits of tiles, broken CDs and ribbons adding colour to the disorienting play of reflections. Rag has rigged up one of the CCTV cameras to a hard disk recorder and each night he stays up till the early hours reciting political speeches dressed in a range of costumes; from drag to *commedia della'arte*, workwear and high fashion, African and Trobriand masks. He delivers Jerry Rubin's speech outside the 1968 Democratic National Convention in Chicago dressed as a Wild Man, the Marquis de Sade's 'Yet Another Effort, Frenchmen, If You Would Become Republicans' in the costume of a petrol station attendant, and the Arabic translation of Valerie Solanas' S.C.U.M. Manifesto dressed as explorer Wilfred Thesiger. His great work is the recitation and recording of the Putney Debates delivered in comic voices, make up and various costumes over the course of eight nights.

Rag spends the daytime lounging on the sofa snorting ketamine and reviewing the previous night's video footage. He thinks of these performances as out of body experience, time travel and a total exorcism of all prior political histories and rituals. While he's laying this material to rest without peace, he's also putting himself through intense fragmentation – a complex and generative game between selves which become increasingly distant and unrecognisable.

For as long as he could remember Rag had detested all forms of theatre and fiction. He could not conceive of a work detached from life. He found any contrivance or artifice meaningless decoration. Now he dwelled intensely upon this hated psychologisation of fictive figures. In his play he aspired to absolute inauthenticity – the matter of making himself an ass in a lion's skin and a king of nothing – pushing the inhabitation of other poses until they are forced, through his body, to impart the real. At present the real was taking the shape of scar tissue forming inside Rag's lungs from the asbestos dropping off the roof of the cave and onto the table where he cut his K. He had made a kind of den built from skipped ceiling tiles – a secondary stage of isolation from the penthouse. On the table he chopped up fat lines of K spelling out the various names for the possible conditions that might in time be responsible for his demise: pulmonary fibrosis, mesotheliomas, asbestosis. It seemed that at this point Rag had found a way out. An end of sorts.

Anthony Iles <anthony@metamute.org> is a contributing editor to *Mute*

STEGANOGRAPHIA:

Hoc est:

ARS PER OCCULTAM SCRIPTURAM ANIMI SUI VOLUNTATEM ABSENTIBUS

aperiendi certa;

AUTHORE

REVERENDISSIMO ET CLARISSIMO VIRO,

JOANNE TRITHEMIO, Abbate Spanhaimensi, &

Magiæ Naturalis Magistro perfectissimo.

PRÆFIXA EST HUIC OPERI SUA CLAVIS, SEU vera introductio ab ipso Authore concinnata;

HACTENUS QUIDEM A MULTIS MULTUM DESIderata, sed à paucissimis visa:

Nunc vero in gratiam secretioris Philosophiæ Studiosorum publici iuris facta.

Cum Privilegio & consensu Superiorum.

FRANCOFURTI,

Ex Officina Typographica MATTHIÆ BECKERI, Sumptibus IOANNIS BERNERI.

Anno M. DC. VI.

Steganographia by Martin Howse

المجاهد التقني
مجلة دورية تصدر عن مركز الفجر للإعلام
العدد الثاني لشهر صفر، سنة ١٤٢٨ هجرية
٢
كيف تخفي معلوماتك داخل صورك
سلسلة شرح الفيديو (ج٢)
ترجمة الأفلام عن طريق العناوين الجانبية
كيف تنشئ موقعا جهاديا من الألف الى الياء (ج١)
برنامج أسرار المجاهدين رؤية من الداخل
الأسلحة الذكية : صواريخ أرض جو
الفجر

```
00000000  4e 4f 54 49 46 59 20 2a  20 48 54 54 50 2f 31 2e NOTIFY *  HTTP/1.
00000010  31 0d 0a 48 4f 53 54 3a  20 32 33 39 2e 32 35 35 1..HOST:  239.255
00000020  2e 32 35 35 2e 32 35 30  3a 31 39 30 30 0d 0a 43 .255.250 :1900..C
00000030  41 43 48 45 2d 43 4f 4e  54 52 4f 4c 3a 20 6d 61 ACHE-CON TROL: ma
00000040  78 2d 61 67 65 3d 31 38  30 30 0d 0a 4c 4f 43 41 x-age=18 00..LOCA
00000050  54 49 4f 4e 3a 20 68 74  74 70 3a 2f 2f 31 39 32 TION: ht tp://192
00000060  2e 31 36 38 2e 32 2e 31  30 34 3a 31 30 32 34 32 .168.2.1 04:10242
00000070  2f 64 65 73 63 72 69 70  74 69 6f 6e 2e 78 6d 6c /descrip tion.xml
00000080  0d 0a 4e 54 3a 20 75 75  69 64 3a 75 70 6e 70 5f ..NT: uu id:upnp_
00000090  4e 65 74 77 6f 72 6b 43  61 6d 65 72 61 57 69 74 NetworkC ameraWit
000000A0  68 50 61 6e 54 69 6c 74  2d 30 30 30 32 44 31 30 hPanTilt -0002D10
000000B0  33 33 33 33 46 0d 0a 4e  54 53 3a 20 73 73 64 70 3333F..N TS: ssdp
000000C0  3a 61 6c 69 76 65 0d 0a  53 45 52 56 45 52 3a 20 :alive.. SERVER: 
000000D0  45 6d 62 65 64 64 65 64  20 55 50 6e 50 2f 31 2e Embedded  UPnP/1.
000000E0  30 0d 0a 55 53 4e 3a 20  75 75 69 64 3a 75 70 6e 0..USN:  uuid:upn
000000F0  70 5f 4e 65 74 77 6f 72  6b 43 61 6d 65 72 61 57 p_Networ kCameraW
00000100  69 74 68 50 61 6e 54 69  6c 74 2d 30 30 30 32 44 ithPanTi lt-0002D
00000110  31 30 33 33 33 33 46 0d  0a 0d 0a                103333F. ...
0000011B  4e 4f 54 49 46 59 20 2a  20 48 54 54 50 2f 31 2e NOTIFY *  HTTP/1.
0000012B  31 0d 0a 48 4f 53 54 3a  20 32 33 39 2e 32 35 35 1..HOST:  239.255
0000013B  2e 32 35 35 2e 32 35 30  3a 31 39 30 30 0d 0a 43 .255.250 :1900..C
0000014B  41 43 48 45 2d 43 4f 4e  54 52 4f 4c 3a 20 6d 61 ACHE-CON TROL: ma
0000015B  78 2d 61 67 65 3d 31 38  30 30 0d 0a 4c 4f 43 41 x-age=18 00..LOCA
0000016B  54 49 4f 4e 3a 20 68 74  74 70 3a 2f 2f 31 39 32 TION: ht tp://192
0000017B  2e 31 36 38 2e 32 2e 31  30 34 3a 31 30 32 34 32 .168.2.1 04:10242
0000018B  2f 64 65 73 63 72 69 70  74 69 6f 6e 2e 78 6d 6c /descrip tion.xml
0000019B  0d 0a 4e 54 3a 20 75 72  6e 3a 73 63 68 65 6d 61 ..NT: ur n:schema
000001AB  73 2d 75 70 6e 70 2d 6f  72 67 3a 64 65 76 69 63 s-upnp-o rg:devic
000001BB  65 3a 4e 65 74 77 6f 72  6b 43 61 6d 65 72 61 57 e:Networ kCameraW
000001CB  69 74 68 50 61 6e 54 69  6c 74 3a 31 0d 0a 4e 54 ithPanTi lt:1..NT
000001DB  53 3a 20 73 73 64 70 3a  61 6c 69 76 65 0d 0a 53 S: ssdp: alive..S
000001EB  6d 62 65 64 64 65 64 3a  0a 0a c2 84 68 65 6e 20 mbedded: ....hen 
000001FB  73 68 c2 97 6c 6c 20 74  68 65 20 72 65 c2 97 6c sh..ll t he re..l
0000020B  6d 20 6f 66 20 65 6c c2  98 69 6f 6e 20 47 20 67 m of el. .ion G g
0000021B  6f 6d 65 20 74 6f 20 67  72 65 c2 97 74 20 c2 99 ome to g re..t ..
0000022B  45 52 56 45 52 3a 20 45  6d 62 65 64 64 65 64 20 ERVER: E mbedded 
0000023B  55 50 6e 50 2f 31 2e 30  0d 0a 55 53 4e 3a 20 75 UPnP/1.0 ..USN: u
0000024B  75 69 64 3a 75 70 6e 70  5f 4e 65 74 77 6f 72 6b uid:upnp _Network
0000025B  43 61 6d 65 72 61 57 69  74 68 50 61 6e 54 69 6c CameraWi thPanTil
0000026B  74 2d 30 30 30 32 44 31  30 33 33 33 33 46 0d 0a t-0002D1 03333F..
```

Albion rose from where h
e laboured at the Mill with Slaves giving himself
for the Nations he danc'd the dance of Eternal Death

(a) Original (stegged) image

(b) After processing

Figure 1: Various steganographic detection algorithms

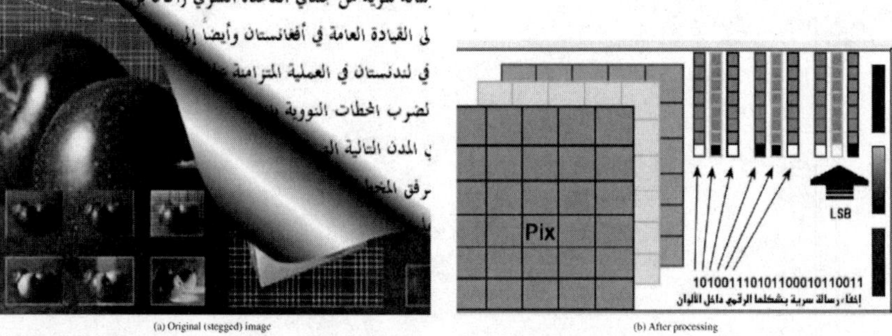

(a) Original (stegged) image

(b) After processing

Figure 2: Various steganographic detection algorithms

NAME

steghide – a steganography program

SYNOPSIS

steghide *command* [*arguments*]

DESCRIPTION

Steghide is a steganography program that is able to hide data in various kinds of image- and audio-files. The color- respectivly sample-frequencies are not changed thus making the embedding resistant against first-order statistical tests.

Features include the compression of the embedded data, encryption of the embedded data and automatic integrity checking using a checksum. The JPEG, BMP, WAV and AU file formats are supported for use as cover file. There are no restrictions on the format of the secret data.

Steghide uses a graph-theoretic approach to steganography. You do not need to know anything about graph theory to use steghide and you can safely skip the rest of this paragraph if you are not interested in the technical details. The embedding algorithm roughly works as follows: At first, the secret data is compressed and encrypted. Then a sequence of postions of pixels in the cover file is created based on a pseudo-random number generator initialized with the passphrase (the secret data will be embedded in the pixels at these positions). Of these positions those that do not need to be changed (because they already contain the correct value by chance) are sorted out. Then a graph-theoretic matching algorithm finds pairs of positions such that exchanging their values has the effect of embedding the corresponding part of the secret data. If the algorithm cannot find any more such pairs all exchanges are actually performed. The pixels at the remaining positions (the positions that are not part of such a pair) are also modified to contain the embedded data (but this is done by overwriting them, not by exchanging them with other pixels). The fact that (most of) the embedding is done by exchanging pixel values implies that the first-order statistics (i.e. the number of times a color occurs in the picture) is not changed. For audio files the algorithm is the same, except that audio samples are used instead of pixels.

The default encryption algorithm is Rijndael with a key size of 128 bits (which is AES – the advanced encryption standard) in the cipher block chaining mode. If you do not trust this combination for whatever reason feel free to choose another algorithm/mode combination (information about all possible algorithms and modes is displayed by the **encinfo** command). The checksum is calculated using the CRC32 algorithm.

COMMANDS

In this section the commands for steghide are listed. The first argument must always be one of these commands. You can supply additional arguments to the **embed**, **extract** and **info** commands. The other commands to not take any arguments.

embed, --embed
: Embed secret data in a cover file thereby creating a stego file.

extract, --extract
: Extract secret data from a stego file.

info, --info
: Display information about a cover or stego file.

encinfo, --encinfo
: Display a list of encryption algorithms and modes that can be used. No arguments required.

version, --version
: Display short version information. No arguments required.

license, --license
: Display steghide's license. No arguments required.

references

- page 1: Steganographia, hoc est, ars per occultam Scripturam... Johannes Trithemius.
- page 2: "Secret Connections - Encrypting Information in Image [Files]" from the second issue of Al-Mujahid Al-Taqni ("The Technical Mujahid") E-Magazine.
- page 3: Albion Drive, Newcastle upon Tyne. Network sniffing using Wireshark conducted during the Courier' Tragedy workshop 2009.
- page 4: image of Villa Alba, former Republic of Salo.
- pages 5 and 6: Pont de l'Alma, Paris steganography/invocation.
- page 7: manual page for steghide, steganography program.

resources

- Steganographia, 1606, Johannes Trithemius
- Technical Mujahid - Issue Two, 2007, Al Fajr Information Center
- Bibliography: http://data-hiding.com/
- Bibliography for text-based steganography: http://semantilog.ucam.org/biblingsteg/
- wbStego: http://wbstego.wbailer.com/
- Stegtunnel (covert channel in the IPID and sequence number fields of any desired TCP connection): http://www.synacklabs.net/projects/stegtunnel/
- Stepic (Python image steganography): http://domnit.org/2007/02/stepic
- Forensic tools: http://unixsadm.blogspot.com/2007/10/digital-forensic-tools-imaging.html
- Text-based steganography: http://www.siefkes.net/software/nlstego/
- http://lcamtuf.coredump.cx/soft/snowdrop.tgz
- http://www.fasterlight.com/hugg/projects/stegparty.html
- http://www.nicetext.com/
- http://www.fourmilab.ch/stego/
- http://1010.co.uk/org/software.html
- Steghide (images) : http://steghide.sourceforge.net/
- Outguess (images): http://www.outguess.org/

```
They sought it with thimbles, they sought it with care;
They pursued it with forks and hope;
They threatened its life with a railway-share;
They charmed it with smiles and soap.
```

HOW NOT TO BE AN ATHEIST

Ben Pritchett dives into the alphabet soup of Brian Rotman's *Becoming Beside Ourselves* and Joanna Zylinska's *Bioethics in the Age of New Media* and picks apart the jumbled relations between ethics, new media and subjectivity

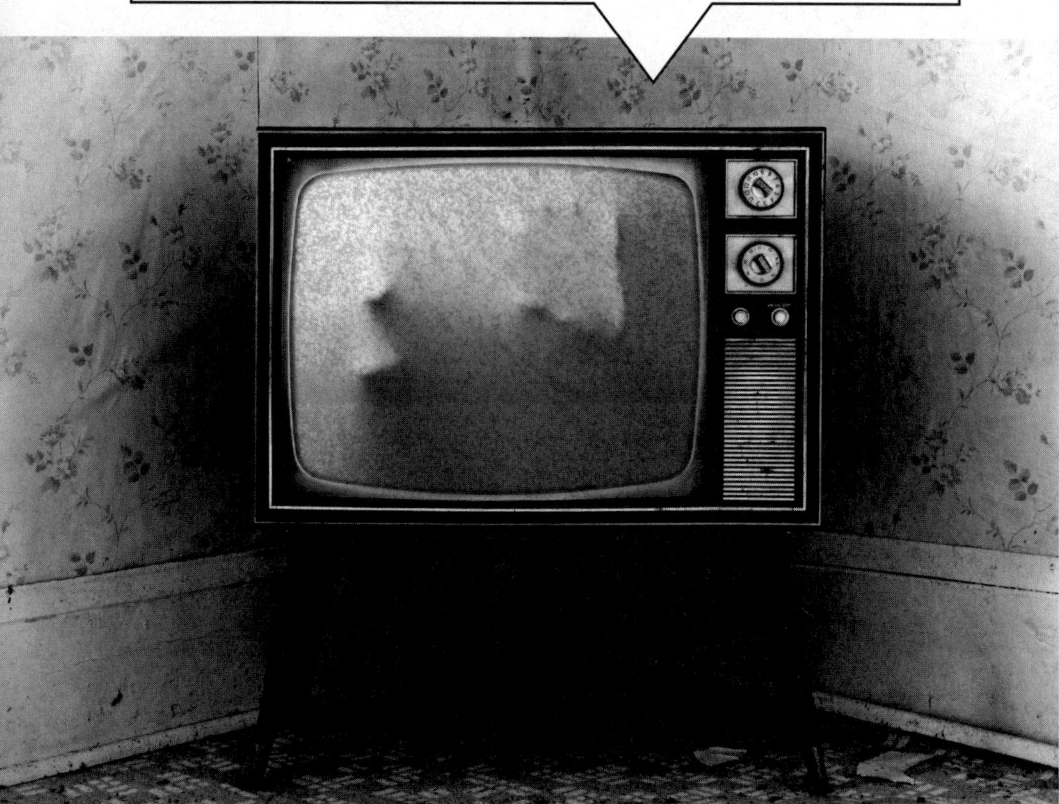

Image: still from David Cronenberg's *Videodrome*, 1983

These books share a concern with the way that 'new media' are changing what it means to be human.

For Rotman, monotheism, and the belief in the soul, are 'media effects', a result of the forcing of human nature to conform to the technology of alphabetic writing (a nature subdued to what it works in, like the dyer's hand). God and the soul, 'ghosts' in Rotman's terminology, are the ideal users which the alphabet seems to presuppose, the kind of agent to which it appears perfectly adapted: but in fact human beings have had to adapt their bodies (even mortify or mutilate themselves) in order to become users of the medium. The ideal user is thus an imaginary projection of the medium, an impossible aspiration given our irreducible materiality. The attempt to transform ourselves into such ghosts causes a great deal of suffering. Now the alphabetic epoch is coming to an end. The rise of new media – particularly motion capture technology – will allow us to express ourselves in new and exciting ways, and the alphabet's decline will also lead to the extinction of God and soul. The 'distributed human being' is the new kind of subjectivity that new media might give rise to. However, in a surprise twist, Rotman proposes that this will not result in an end to supernatural beliefs, but that we will find new, more benevolent ghosts to believe in, more appropriate to the world of new media.

Zylinska's style is more discursive. She begins with a critique of the dominant humanist philosophies of bioethics, which are based on a medical paradigm. She then considers how these could be problematised by drawing on continental philosophy and media/cultural studies. Her intention is to make bioethics more open to animal and technological otherness. Thus while she flirts with an ecological perspective, by way of her consideration of cybernetics, she ends up closer to a rights-and-obligations-based position. She advocates an ethical philosophy based on Levinas' philosophy of Alterity (while doing her best not to alienate fans of Deleuze). She then offers three case studies, in the course of which she continues to expand her theoretical palette: a discussion of the reality TV makeover show, *The Swan*; a consideration of the implications of the popular science discourse around DNA; and a discussion of the body artist Stelarc.

Each writer oscillates between ontological and epistemological arguments. There are two positions, never fully resolved: are new technologies, particularly media, fundamentally transforming (or taking us beyond) what it is to be human, or do they simply reveal that humans were 'always already' constituted by technology? Without a historical framework for their analyses, both writers find themselves led into an apocalyptic rhetoric, ambiguously poised between transfiguration and unveiling. However, they are anxious to assert their atheist principles, and thus each produces a paradoxically humanist eschatology. This may be symptomatic of the horizons of the media studies paradigm.

Rotman breathlessly asserts that:

> The West's ontotheological metaphysics, with its indivisible, unique-unto-themselves and beyond-which-nothing monads of an absolute Truth behind reality and a monolithic transcendent God entity begins to be revealed as a mediological achievement – magnificent but no longer appropriate – of a departing age'.[1]

For Rotman, this brave new epoch not only reveals that 'God' is an antiquated notion, but so is 'mind' and any notion of transcendent human agency. The history of the human species resembles nothing so much as a roller-coaster ride: 'We are living through tumultuous, dizzying times on the cusp of a new era; times spanning a seismic jump in the matrix of human culture'.[2]

Zylinska, on the other hand, wants to assert that history is not running on technological rails, but that, in the final analysis, humanity can still influence the direction of travel – or at the very least, keep various options open. She argues that 'Bioethics, as I have envisaged it [is] a way of cutting through the "flow of life" with a double-edged sword of productive power and infinite responsibility' – a phrase which brings to mind Milton's 'two-handed engine', or the angelic sword guarding the gates of Paradise.[3] For Zylinska, what is needed is to reclaim the transcendent powers of ethical decision from God in the name of (a suitably chastened and tentative) humanity: 'I would like to suggest, that partial assessment of the situation by the human [...] constitutes a (necessarily shaky) foundation of what I have been referring to as "alternative" bioethics.'[4]

the alphabet's decline will also lead to the extinction of God and soul

These two diametrically opposed but both avowedly atheist strategies take as their guiding principles, on Rotman's side, Gilles Deleuze, and on Zylinska's, a post-Derridean, (and therefore Godless, even non-humanist) Emmanuel Levinas. Zylinska notes how the two strands represent divergent philosophical traditions, of 'immanence' and 'transcendence' respectively.[5] It would be possible to see the two books under review as skirmishes in a territory dispute between the two strands of theory. This would be unfortunate, since neither author, disappointingly, does justice to their chosen philosophical reference points.

Rotman pulls no punches in his contempt for Derrida & Co., at one point describing grammatology as,

> 'one of the postmodern branches' according to Vassilis Lambropoulos, 'of the Science of Judaism'; a triumph enshrined in Jacques Derrida's voice-silencing and body-annihilating grammatological mantra 'There is no outside to the text'.[6]

If this sounds anti-semitic, then it should be noted that Rotman is an equal-opportunities insulter of monotheists, observing in one endnote that

> the obligatory gestures and body practices that constitute Islamic worship and indeed define what it means to be a Muslim are far more pronounced than anything resembling them in the other Abrahamic religions and seem, in terms of the inculcation and maintenance of fervent, unshakeable belief, to be correspondingly more effective.[7]

Actually Rotman could learn a lot from Derrida, if he took the time to read him instead of recycling journalistic clichés. *Of Grammatology* offers close readings of an array of canonical texts of Western literature, most of which decry the inadequacy of written language to represent physical presence: this accumulation of sources flatly contradicts Rotman's thesis that 'writing has effaced its own role in constructing the hierarchies of mind over body'.[8] Rotman's notion of 'ghostliness' is also implicitly positioned against the politicised conception explored in Derrida's *Spectres of Marx*: for Rotman, ghosts are 'distinct from spectres such as individual revenants demanding, like the ghost of Hamlet's father, retribution, revenge and the righting of wrongs, or from identifiable sites of social repression and invisibilization'.[9]

One of the weaknesses of alphabetic writing, according to Rotman, is the fact that it promotes 'serialism'.[10] His linear narrative partakes in the very same logic. He even heads a series of subsections 'gesture -> speech', 'speech -> writing', and 'writing -> networks' without an apparent sense of irony.[11] The book reads like a giant 'liar's paradox' – his argument is that the alphabet conceals its own negative effects. So either the alphabet will prevent us from being convinced of the book's message, or we will accept the book's message, immediately refuting it in practice.

Of course the logic of the alphabet is not 'deeply and inescapably serial', 'isolated, independent and indivisible' as Rotman claims.[12] On the contrary, it facilitates random access and cross-referencing, as his bizarrely self-defeating examples of the encyclopaedia and the library demonstrate. Similarly 'the word' is not 'stable, integral, fixed, discrete, enclosing a unique, interior meaning' – it is deeply ironic that Rotman feels the need to multiply adjectives in order to say one supposedly simple thing here.[13] If further proof were needed that writing can accommodate parallelism, overdetermination, multiple causality, etc., it would be worth reading Bakhtin on novelistic discourse, Empson on ambiguity and Barthes on textuality.

Rotman is remarkably single-minded in his assault on God by way of the alphabet, and thus his philosophical sources are pared down to the point of travesty in order to support his central thesis. This results in a depoliticised Deleuze – it's hard to believe that Rotman is citing the same writer who co-wrote a critique of capitalism from the perspective of schizophrenia. For Rotman, 'writing' is the agent that has enjoyed a 'three millennia hegemony', and the pressing political problem of our time is not capitalist imperialism but 'literacy's increasing colonization of all that was the province of oralism'.[14] '[D]ivision of labour', for Rotman, is not an economic relation of power between social groups, classes or nations, but a functional split within the brain, between 'limbic systems' and 'neocortex', and the midbrain takes

Image: Eine, design for Phillip Font

the place of the 'disenfranchised and repressed'.[15] Rotman even retains the Marxist categories of base and superstructure, but now the 'base' is reduced to 'reading and writing'.[16] Rotman seems to have missed Deleuze and Guattari's key point about conflicting regimes of signs, which is that 'there is more to the picture than semiotic systems waging war on one another armed only with their own weapons. *Very specific assemblages of power impose signifiance and subjectification* as their determinate form of expression'.[17]

Rotman's argument is appealingly elegant, but the weaknesses are an inevitable result of such elegance. If we deny the existence of God, only to posit a single material cause in His place, then 'atheism' will represent no advance towards a materialist understanding of history and society. Rotman argues that 'an entire neurological apparatus [was] brought into being by the alphabet in order for it to function' – we might compare the function of the alphabet in Rotman's theory with that of the 'selfish gene' in Dawkins'.[18]

we might compare the function of the alphabet in Rotman's theory with that of the 'selfish gene' in Dawkins'

Rotman's neglect of international politics (or the world system) is symptomatic of a more general problem of his Anglophone/Eurocentric point of view. It is not clear that Rotman has sufficient knowledge of comparative religion to make his case for a unique tie between phonetic writing and monotheism. His theory is unable to explain how and why monotheism arose in ancient Egypt – this is an inconvenient fact, and he argues that Egyptian monotheism was unsustainable without phonetic writing. There also seems to be some debate as to whether the early Han Chinese worship of Shangdi could be considered a form of 'monotheism'. I am not able to assess the validity of this argument, but it is notable that Rotman does not even mention the inconvenient possibility, which would falsify his theory.

Rotman's lack of cross-cultural awareness is matched by a historical insensitivity with regard to 'The West' itself. At the origin of 'Western civilization' Rotman cannot explain why different 'ghosts' arose in the Greek and Jewish belief systems, because, for him, alphabetic writing overrides all other characteristics. Rotman's linking of new media with the death of God is also unable to account for atheist movements which arose during the alphabetic epoch. Greek atheism, enlightenment rationalism and revolutionary socialist refutations of God are not considered. Of the three best-known atheists in history, Rotman does not even mention Marx or Nietzsche, and only invokes Freud in a footnote, to criticise him for arguing that Jewish monotheism descended from Egyptian monotheism. It seems gratuitous to say it, but all of these arguments were disseminated textually. And, as far as the present moment goes, Rotman can only explain the rise of fundamentalism as a desperate last-gasp backlash of the alphabetic God against his inevitable demise.

I have not addressed mathematics here. Rotman's earlier texts were concerned with the semiotics of mathematics rather than the alphabet. His 'interlude' on 'technologized mathematics' in this book seems to be a holdover from his earlier work, and he is somewhat apologetic for it. As someone with a background in literary studies, I do not feel I can tackle Rotman's argument on its own terms here. There might be some grist for a philosopher of mathematics to compare Rotman's take on the concept of infinity with the philosophy of Alain Badiou, since both writers assert that their reading of this branch of mathematics is fundamentally atheist; however, as far as I can see, their arguments are diametrically opposed.

Zylinska wants (a chastened) humanity to reclaim the transcendent powers of ethical decision from God

Zylinska comes closest to Rotman's field of interest in her discussion of the discourse around DNA as a 'secret code'. This overlaps with his discussion of computing and of Alan Turing, the celebrated code-breaker. However, Zylinska situates this discourse far more explicitly in the context of cryptography and the military-industrial complex. This characterises the great value of Zylinska's book, as opposed to Rotman's: Zylinska is open to questions of politics and economics. She is aware that whilst technology, and media in particular, does change possibilities for forms of subjectivity, this technological aspect is circumscribed and overdetermined by wider systems. Zylinska is well versed in the Derridean deconstructive tradition, and thus does not attack writing per se, recognising that many qualities of new media were always already present in writing, so, for example 'linking, brought to the fore in online texts, is always already the condition of linear, grammatological writing'.[19] Thus, pace Rotman, individualism is not an effect of 'writing', but of (neo)liberal economics: the 'dominant politico-ethical models in the capitalist world, where the relationality of living beings is overlooked for the analyses of monadic entities, and at the expense of the forgetting of flesh, of sex, of sexual difference'.[20] This allows Zylinska to indicate why, in spite of an increasingly networked society, people feel ever more atomised, a problem which Rotman completely fails to address.

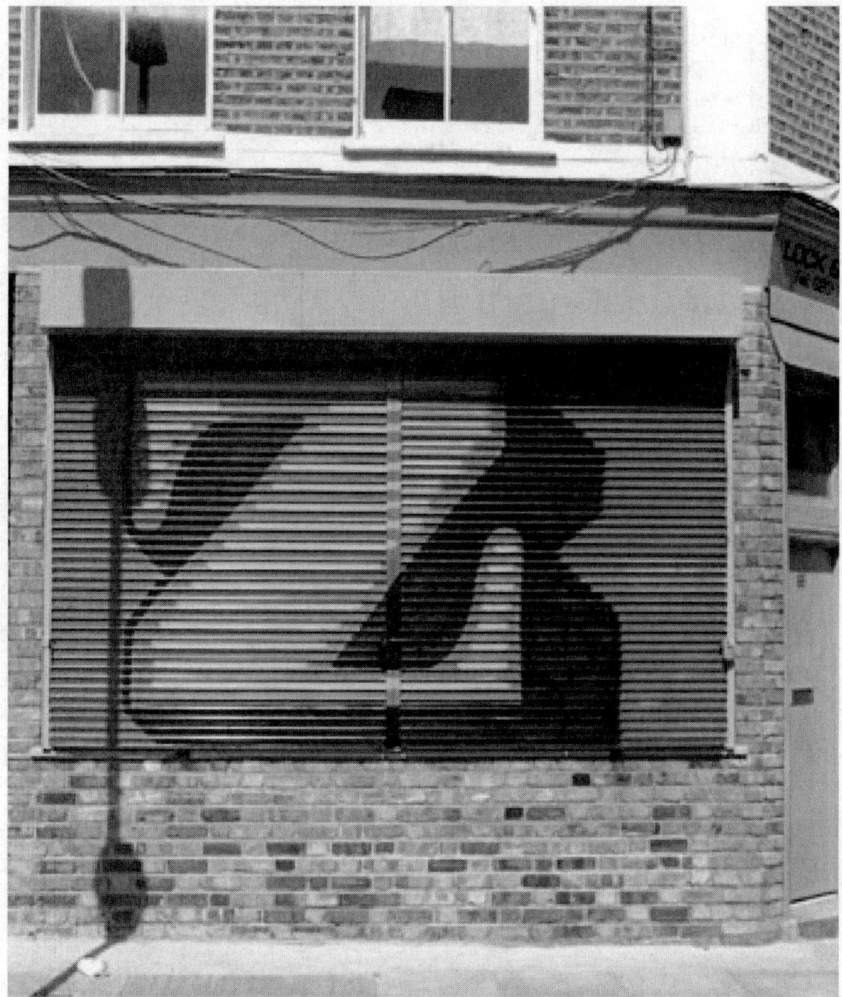

Image: Eine, shutter front graffiti, East London

The ideological illusion of finding one's 'true self' undergoes a materialist deconstruction in Zylinska's analysis of the Fox TV programme *The Swan*, where the self is shown to be a construction which partakes of human, machinic and animal elements. This mystificatory programme is implicitly contrasted with the 'Bioart' of Stelarc, which Zylinska argues offers an emancipatory revelation of human situatedness in technical and animal networks. While acknowledging the conditioning effects of technology, Zylinska shows, against a technological determinism, that new media might become technologies of domination rather than freedom, and the way in which things will develop depends on concrete ethical decisions.

Zylinska is rather eclectic in her use of theories, and does not attempt to deny their diverse and irreducible singularity. (Incidentally, her sense of the word 'singular' varies depending upon which theory she is using – sometimes it is a synonym for 'individual', at other times, it means 'unique', in the sense of a one-off event, which may be a social encounter). Her summaries of different theoretical positions are very clear and cogent – the book is a great way to brush up on your biopolitics, with neat encapsulations of Foucault and Agamben, for example. Zylinska is clearly very well read - I was particularly impressed by the positions of Rosi Braidotti and Krzysztof Ziarek, as she summarised them here, and I intend to investigate them further.

If such dog-versus-scallop standoffs arose repeatedly, I would begin to question my sanity

Unlike Rotman, Zylinska is conciliatory towards her philosophical rivals: 'my book is by no means positioned as anti-Deleuzian'.[21] It appears that we are meant to understand that the 'productive power' of her 'double-edged sword' comes from Deleuze, while the 'infinite responsibility' is bequeathed to her by Levinas. Unfortunately, a rapprochement between these two philosophers in Zylinska's terms seems unlikely, since her argument is premised on the questionable assertion that Levinas provides the theory of subjectivity and agency that Deleuze lacks. This seems to be a reaction to a predominant 'Deleuzianism', as noted above with respect to Rotman, which has been purged of its critical aspects. But Deleuze and Guattari did theorise subjectivity, in their analysis of the difference between subject groups and subjugated groups (in *Anti-Oedipus*). The problem for Zylinska, it seems, is not that Deleuze lacks a theory of subjectivity per se, but that he lacks an individualist, and dare I say it, humanist theory of subjectivity.

Zylinska fails to give a plausible account of the way in which the two philosophical positions represented by Deleuze and Levinas could complement each other. There is very little in common between the way that Deleuze and Guattari argue, in 'Year O: Faciality', that faces are produced by a (racist) authoritarian/despotic 'abstract machine', and the way that Levinas makes the face of the Other the transcendent starting point of his ethics. This is not a productive combination; it is necessary to choose between the different stances that these incommensurable philosophies represent.

Zylinska's theoretical generosity tends towards a pose of absolute impartiality. It is a shame, because she is very attentive to those factors of politics, economics, gender and race which Rotman omitted. Thus, rather than seeing the unjustly enshrined user of technology as a truly disembodied ghost, Zylinska critiques the way that, in 'traditional' bioethics, '"the average white middle-class man in the street" remains [...] a measuring stick against which ethical injustice carried out against women is judged.'[22] In other words, these privileged male individuals are not genuinely pure minds, but they are able to pose as 'disembodied rational subject[s]' and remain unconscious of their particular kind of embodiment because the social system accommodates it by default.[23] But in the final analysis Zylinska's empiricism is negated by the fact that she champions the ethical nature of a 'content-free obligation', towards a '(formal not theological) elsewhere' and asserts that 'undecideability [...] arguably, is a key condition of ethics'.[24]

I hope Zylinska is indulging in self-parody when she argues, for example, that

> [t]he nature and significance of the ethical difference between, for example, "abusing a dog and abusing a scallop" will nevertheless have to be responsibly decided always anew, in particular contexts, networks and environments we will find ourselves in, and with all the knowledge and affect we will be able to mobilize.[25]

Though it seems redundant to say it, I hope I never have to choose between abusing a dog and abusing a scallop. Should I be forced into such a diabolical dilemma, I don't think I would regret unthinkingly siding with the dog, even if some people might feel that I was acting on the basis of 'moralistic' prejudices rather than an 'ethical' decision. If such dog-versus-scallop standoffs arose repeatedly, in a variety of 'contexts, networks and environments' I would begin to question my sanity.

Zylinska's non-judgemental position is less amusing when, having constructed an elaborate Agamben-influenced analogy between the Fox TV makeover show *The Swan* and the Nazi concentration camps, she protests that

> I realize there may be something rather frustrating about a bioethics that refuses to evaluate the morality of the actions in which the producers, participants, and audiences of the radical makeover show The Swan are engaged.[26]

The implied argument up to this point was clear – American imperialism, (post-9/11, at least), is quasi-fascist, and the Fox network is a propaganda machine. Does Zylinska really believe she can make such an analogy and yet not imply a negative evaluation of the show, or influence her readers to reach the same conclusion? Surely she is being disingenuous? If not, she really ought to go the extra mile and draw some explicit inferences from her analysis. (For the record, I think the show sounds pretty depressing. But putting a stop to *The Swan* is not very high on my list of ethico-political priorities).

Image: still from David Cronenberg's *Videodrome*, 1983

Both writers produce versions of their philosophical sources which are rather unethical. I do not feel that either of them fully takes on the challenge of their dominant theoretical borrowings, Deleuze or Derrida. In neither book does the use of theory support a strong atheist position. My acquaintance with the discourse of Media Studies is limited, but it seems that there may be something inherent to the way that the questions are framed by this discipline that necessitates a form of (theologically inflected) humanism. This distorts the philosophies taken up, and leads to a regression from the radical, though very different positions advanced by Deleuze and Derrida.

Taking the position of devil's advocate, I would like to suggest that it is no coincidence that one of the founding texts of Media Studies, *Understanding Media*, was written by a Catholic humanist, and subtitled 'The Extensions of Man'. McLuhan trained in the English literary tradition at Cambridge, under F.R. Leavis, who is (in) famous for his nostalgia for the 'organic society', and his role in the Two Cultures controversy with C.P. Snow. Whereas McLuhan criticised the (Protestant) 'Gutenberg galaxy' of the printing press from a Catholic point of view, Rotman wants to criticise writing itself from an atheist point of view. However, he still partakes of the old organicist rhetoric, albeit clad in a dubiously 'neuroscientific' garb.

There are moments when Rotman's argument reads like a restatement of T.S. Eliot's lament over the 'dissociation of sensibility'. Rotman, for example, describes the arrival of new media as causing the 'coming apart of a previously self-sufficient and seamless whole. The result in each case is a *dissociation* which restructures consciousness'.[27] At times Rotman suggests that this disrupted unity was only ever an illusion: 'every medium disrupts what had been for its predecessor *conceived as* a seamless whole'.[28] But his account of the effects of the alphabet does not seem to be a description of the irruption of reality into an imaginary unity. Rather his language implies something ontologically fundamental: what he calls a 'transcendental fissure' or, indeed, a 'pre-frontal lobotomy'.[29] This is more than a superficial rhetorical problem. The conceptual vocabulary which structures the discourse of both these books, at a deep level, partakes of the same difficulty.

The first problem relates to technology. Both Zylinska and Rotman are in agreement that technology plays a part in determining what actions we are capable of: it does not simply extend or circumscribe a natural human condition, but is implicated in the production and constitution of the human. But neither writer is able to consistently sustain this avowed position. By using the term 'technology' there is already a danger of reifying an object. It is for this reason that Raymond Williams, in his study of *Television*, preferred to discuss individual technologies in the context of broader 'cultural forms' – ensembles of social processes and mutually reinforcing technologies. Rotman falls at the first hurdle here: his all-consuming fixation with the negative characteristics of the alphabet participates in the very 'fetishism' that he claims to decry: '*Jahweh*'s self-birth from within alphabetic writing at the site of the written 'I' left in its wake an intense and lasting alphabetic fetishism within Jewish mystical and philosophical thought'.[30]

Both writers produce versions of their philosophical sources which are rather unethical

Furthermore, although both writers draw on theories that address general questions of technology, their specific area of interest is 'media'. By narrowing the focus from 'technology' per se, to 'media', there is an inevitable foregrounding of those particular kinds of technology that operate *between people*, producing human bodies, affects and subjectivity, i.e. individual and collective human life. This narrowing of attention leads to a neglect of those technologies which produce physical products like commodities or public works. It also marginalises consideration of those technologies which are directed against other people with violent intent. In other words, by zeroing in on 'media', Rotman and Zylinska tend to marginalise technologies directed towards an objective outside, or against outsiders: 'tools' on the one hand, and 'weapons' on the other. A theory of media is necessarily much narrower than a general theory of technology, or of machines, which would encompass all these types. So in both books, technological questions relating to economics, warfare, and even politics are given little space – always with the caveat that Zylinska is more open to acknowledge the limitations of her discourse, and look beyond it. This tends to undermine the avowed goal of each author to advance a materialist, atheist and non-humanist position. One can imagine a 'machine' which is directed towards a non-anthropomorphic other, but it is much more difficult to conceive of a 'medium' which would be.

Nevertheless, even within this broad horizon of humanism, it seems an unfortunate result that each writer should (against their avowed intentions) fall back into individualism, rather than a social theory. Again, Raymond Williams' attendance to vocabulary is helpful here: he noted that the term 'medium' is another reification, and that we would be better off talking about 'social practices' (in *Marxism and Literature*). The word 'medium' almost inevitably implies a third term mediating between two individual actors. Thus for Rotman the guiding empirical paradigm is the cognitive neuroscience of discrete brains, implying interiority and possessive individualism ('activity in the body of the user'; 'technologies of parallelism [...] reconfigure the thought diagrams inside (as we still say) our heads').[31] For Zylinska, bioethics is based on the 'narcissistic' relation of self and other: 'an act of reaching to other [...] is narcissistic, but also that narcissism is revealed as necessary to establishing this relationship'.[32]

My initial feeling, reading Zylinska after Rotman, was a sense of relief in her return to concretely situated cases, and the way that she openly named the powerful forces which anybody trying to act ethically quickly comes up against. But I was ultimately disappointed as she fell back on what I can only call a more humble egocentrism:

> the question whether this ethics also applies to others – other humans but perhaps also apes, dolphins, or even 'intelligent machines' – is not really important because *it only ever applies to me*. It is *my* anxiety about death and *my* awareness of my own mortality that establish a temporality for me while also opening up a set of possibilities.[33]

Zylinska signals her anxiety about this move by her apologetic protests that she is 'not bringing back humanism'.[34] Her capitulation belies the virtues of her critique of previous models of bioethics. As she had correctly argued, the conditions of human agency are trans-individual and trans-human. This seems, indeed, to be the basis of her favourable account of Stelarc's bioart: the aesthetic precedes the ethical, because it makes the trans-individual and trans-human (i.e. social) formation of subjectivity visible. It does not seem to me that any 'decision' is necessary before drawing the logical conclusions of this insight: any active, ethical agency must necessarily be trans-individual and trans-human too, or it will exclude the very forces from which it derives its power. Thus, contra Levinas, ethics do not precede, but follow upon, social and political participation – bearing in mind that 'society' can no longer be circumscribed by a preconceived, organic notion of the human.

Perhaps I will be accused of impatience – naïvely believing that if we can stop using the language and discursive forms of possessive individualism and theology, then we can make our problems disappear. But it is only through the construction and consistent application of a set of concepts adequate to the potentials (but not the inevitabilities) of new technical and social formations, that we will be able to articulate the necessary alliances for an emancipatory socialist project.

Info:

Joanna Zylinska, *Bioethics in the Age of New Media*, London: MIT Press, 2009.

Brian Rotman, *Becoming Beside Ourselves: The Alphabet, Ghosts and Distributed Human Being*, Durham, NC: Duke University Press, 2008.

Footnotes:

1 Brian Rotman, *Becoming Beside Ourselves: The Alphabet, Ghosts and Distributed Human Being*, Durham, NC: Duke University Press, 2008, p. 9.
2 Ibid., p. 105.
3 Joanna Zylinska, *Bioethics in the Age of New Media*, London: MIT Press, 2009, p. 179.
4 Ibid., p. 164.
5 Ibid., p. 30.
6 Rotman, op. cit., p. 124.
7 Ibid., p. 141.
8 Ibid., p. 126.
9 Ibid., p. 113.
10 Ibid., p. 83.
11 Ibid., p. 109-110.
12 Ibid., p. 93.
13 Ibid., p. 95.
14 Ibid., pp. 4 and 30.
15 Ibid., pp. 30 and 31.
16 Ibid., p. 136.
17 Gilles Dezeuze and Felix Guattari, *A Thousand Plateaus*, London: Continuum, 2004, p. 200. Italics in original.
18 Rotman, op. cit., p. 82.
19 Zylinska, op. cit., p. 92.
20 Ibid., pp. 139-140.
21 Ibid., p. x.
22 Ibid., p. 16.
23 Ibid.
24 Ibid., pp. 121, 30 and 52.
25 Ibid., p. 53.
26Ibid., p. 123.
27 Rotman, op. cit., p. 112. My Italics.
28 Ibid., p. 25. My Italics
29 Ibid., pp. 54 and 31..
30 Ibid., 123.
31 Ibid., pp., 82 and 103.
32 Zylinska, op. cit., p. 88.
33 Ibid., 62. Italics in original.
34 Ibid., 53.

Ben Pritchett <PritchettBen@googlemail.com> is an unemployed Oxbridge graduate, who turns down unpaid internships out of necessity rather than choice. He finished his MPhil thesis on Raymond Williams' novel *Second Generation* in June 2009. He works on video documentaries when he gets the chance.

HUNG, DRAWN AND 'QUARTERED'?

Two recently published books – Anna Minton's *Ground Control* and This is Not a Gateway's *Critical Cities* – take stock of the accumulated effects of New Labour's 'urban renaissance'. In his double review, Owen Hatherley sees the tired politics of micro-resistance go head-to-head with some much needed materialist geography

Irrespective of its courting of suburbia, New Labour was very much an urban party. Its bases remained in ex-industrial cities, and its hierarchy was drawn from North London, Greater Manchester and Edinburgh. The Tories, despite their capture of the Greater London Authority, are essentially an outer-suburban and rural party, so it will be instructive to find out what they plan to do with one of the major Blairite shibboleths – the 'urban renaissance'. Coined in the late 1990s by either Ricky Burdett, Anne Power or Richard Rogers, under the auspices of John Prescott and the Urban Task Force, this has become the emblematic term of a middle class return to the cities, and an attendant redevelopment of previously demonised urban spaces. Often this is associated with a particular kind of urban paraphernalia. In terms of architectural artefacts, the urban renaissance has meant lottery funded 'centres', entertainment venues and shopping/eating complexes, clustered around disused river-fronts (Salford Quays, Cardiff Bay, the Tyneside ensemble of Baltic, Sage and Millennium Bridge); in housing, 'mixed use' blocks of flats on brownfield sites, the privatisation of council estates, the reuse of old mills or factories; extensive public art, whether cheerful or enigmatically Gormleyesque, usually symbolising an area's phoenix-like re-emergence; districts become branded 'quarters'; and, perhaps most curiously, piazzas (or, in the incongruously grandiose planning parlance, 'public realm') appear, with attendant coffee concessions, promising to bring European sophistication to Derby or Portsmouth.

tower blocks proposed for the Dalston site, are apparently an 'alien typology', which will be news to many in Hackney

Image: Urban farming against regen? *The Dalston Mill*. Re-staging of Agnes Denes' wheatfield in Manhattan, for the Barbican's Radical Nature exhibition, July 2009

Image: Building development at Dalston Junction, London

The process is partial and unevenly scattered, but reaches its most spectacular stretch in the miles of luxury flats in the former London Docks, the new high-rise skyline of Leeds, the privatised retail district of Liverpool One, or the repopulation of central Manchester. Irrespective of the virtues or otherwise of these new spaces, this urban renaissance is widely considered to have ended in aforementioned city centre flats sitting empty, as if the exodus from the suburbs to the cities was a failed confidence trick. It has left behind half-finished, empty or cheaply-let towers in Glasgow, Stratford or Sheffield which stand both as symbols of the euphemistic 'credit crunch', or the failure, as suburban boosterism might have it, of an attempt to cajole people into a form of living alien to British predilections (although the linked subprime crash in the USA was a suburban rather than inner city phenomenon). The two books under review here attempt to offer some kind of reckoning with the urban renaissance. Anna Minton's *Ground Control – Fear and Happiness in the* 21st *Century*

City sets out to systematically describe a paranoid, privatised new landscape, while This Is Not A Gateway's *Critical Cities – Ideas, Knowledge and Agitation from Emerging Urbanists,* edited by an academic and a 'regeneration professional', Deepa Naik and Trenton Oldfield, offers a rather more impressionistic approach. In both cases we appear to be dealing with former believers in the urban renaissance who have been gradually disappointed by the failures of Blairite urbanism. Gentrifiers against gentrification, we could say. Nonetheless, the difference between the relative force and sophistication of the critiques in these two books is wide indeed.

worryingly academics, planners,architects and urbanists are still terrified by the idea of large-scale planning

This is Not A Gateway describes itself as an 'urban platform', and this is their first anthology. Although they are at pains to stress how inclusive and interdisciplinary the platform is, with contributions showing an impressive range, from aesthetics to health, from art to gardening, the book is mostly derived from various 'salons' at Dalston's Cafe Oto – so many contributions are reviews of or summaries from meetings to which the reader will not have been privy. This tension between an insider perspective and an ostentatious, outreaching friendliness runs throughout *Critical Cities*. There is also a tension among the contributors between those who are genuinely 'critical' of recent policy and those who have, frankly, created, administered and apologised for it from the off. This is obvious from two of the book's several introductions. First, we have a preface from Jemma Basham of the Homes and Communities Agency, the quango that is the successor to the Housing Corporation and the part-privatisation sponsors English Partnerships. Basham works for the 'HCA Academy', about whom the byline optimistically notes that 'its current priority is to give people tools and know-how to deal with the recession and prepare themselves for the upturn'. The HCA also recently bailed out property developers to the tune of £2.8 billion, and is headed by Sir Bob Kerslake, who demolished a prodigious amount of council housing in his time as (unelected) boss of Sheffield City Council and, as *Critical Cities* is 'made possible with the support of the Homes and Communities Agency', one should expect any critique of these policies to be muted or non-existent. Basham's brief but reiterated point is cohesion, consensus, the importance of everyone coming together during the recession, a Keep Calm and Carry On rhetoric which will recur in other contributions. The next introduction is by none other than 'Ricky' Burdett, alleged coiner of the very term 'urban renaissance'. 'City-thinking *for* City-building' is his subject here (the italics are Burdett's). It's a resolutely uncontroversial plea for interdisciplinarity and concrete intervention in the midst of the threats of climate change and the global (if not necessarily national) expansion of cities. Anything non-'inclusive' is lurking below the surface rather than explicitly stated – the insistence that 'global cities' remain 'competitive', or the praise of 'leadership' and 'big-city mayors' in Bogota and elsewhere.

What exactly is the critique offered in *Critical Cities*? The phraseology used by the editors differs, at times, rather radically from the affirmationism of the urban renaissance. Their very name, evoking that curiously suburban New Labour non-plan, the 'Thames Gateway', sounds like a critique of recent planning policy. Here we also find not only the lately deeply unfashionable notion of the 'critical', but the possibility of 'agitation', and the idea that urban issues are worth getting angry about. This is laudable enough, and Oldfield & Naik attempt to sum up the process of gentrification and enclosure with the phrase 'erase, stretch, relinquish'. The example used will be familiar to many *Mute* readers – the Dalston Junction regeneration scheme, where first the existing Georgian and Victorian landscape was erased, the units in the replacement luxury flats were 'stretched', and, when sold off to buy-to-let landlords, the developers of the site will no doubt 'relinquish'. This is a fair summation, and it cannot be pointed out often enough that schemes like Dalston Junction are emphatically not in the interest of the local 'community' (to use the Blairite term invoked as an uncritical good on almost every page in both of these books).

Still, there is occasionally something unsatisfying about a critique of this sort, something peculiarly retrograde: an English Heritage form of community activism. The solicitor Bill Parry-Davies' contribution entails a critique of the Dalston Junction scheme and an explanation of the legal architecture underpinning such grand regeneration projects, along with advocacy on behalf of OPEN Dalston, the group which has attempted to stop the demolition of a venue, shops and housing in favour of two tower blocks (neither of which will include 'affordable' housing) as part of a Transport for London 'hub'. It is useful and politically astute, yet the invocation of 'heritage' is hardly unambiguous. Tower blocks, such as those proposed for the Dalston site, are apparently an 'alien typology', which will be news to the many in Hackney who have lived in them for the last half-century. Consider the likely effect if Hackney Council were to acquiesce in the proposed renovation and cleaning of the area's Georgian properties and the Four Aces nightclub – a heritage showpiece ten minutes from the Square Mile, which might just be more of a draw to the affluent than two towers of Barratt's micro-flats. It has the potential to be a new Covent Garden or Portobello, ready for resettling and cleansing. A positive proposal that didn't involve the patching up of substandard Georgiana was conspicuous by its absence. Re-used old space is as much, if not more of a feature of gentrification than new space, but this interests the contributors rather less. Everyone hates a tower block, after all.

The contributors often seem to have a very particular idea about where the urban renaissance went wrong – through the repetition of the 'mistakes of the 1960s', in the form of modernist architecture and high-rise towers. Lea Ayoub's 'Public Air Space – Planning and Accessing Tall Buildings in London' is a straightforward critique of the high-rise offices and flats that have made a tentative return to the capital over the last decade. She writes that 'before this building boom, the main local experience and reference for tall buildings were those of the 1960s and 1970s, which have been mostly relegated to the periphery and generally convey an image of housing and planning failure and social exclusion', and approvingly quotes Jane Jacobs on modernism as the 'rape of cities'. Now, irrespective of the accuracy or otherwise of this blanket moral judgement in which either something as successful as Pimlico's Churchill Gardens or as cheap and nasty as Canning Town's Freemasons Estate becomes part of the same failed experiment, there is a worthwhile point here. For developers, there is a certain historical obstacle to the neoliberal high-rise city in the form of the immediate revulsion brought on by the memory of sink estates and serried ranks of prole-containing towers, which the 'iconic' design of City skyscrapers (Gherkin, soon to be followed by 'Walkie-Talkie', 'Shard' et al) attempts to circumvent, transforming stacked trading floors into fodder for tourist snapshots.

a slave who 'creatively' 'subverts' space is still a slave

This hostility to modernism and to planning also features in Alan Thompson's two essays here on health in cities, where he outlines the modernist failings of Northwick Park NHS hospital (most notably, it was lamentably uninterested in 'beauty'), and gives '60s hospitals' architecturally inept and wildly expensive exurban PFI replacements an inexplicably easy ride. Aside from its complicity with the demolition of postwar modernist estates, schools or NHS hospitals and their replacement with the Private Finance Initiative, City Academies and Public-Private 'mixed communities', what is really worrying in this reiterated argument is the fact that academics, planners, architects and urbanists are still clearly terrified by the idea of large-scale planning, of new space, of any kind of architecture which is not 'in keeping' with the heritage city, as if fearing they might find themselves demonised as 'social engineers', much as they were in the 1970s and '80s. We do have critiques of the expensive and privatised nature of high-rise towers, and in the case of Louis Moreno's essay here on the 'architecture' of the financial crisis, this can be politically cogent and insightful. Yet there's no critique of the most notable urban artefact of the 'urban renaissance' in London – the four to eight storey blocks of yuppiedromes, built on brownfield site or former council estate, with shops (or Estate Agent) on the ground floor and 'public realm' as sops to the planning officers – an urban typology which is both extremely common and frequently privatised or gated, but whose low-rise nature and brick and/or render and/or wood cladding is presumably less offensive to heritage sensibilities. Either way, it is a shame that planners and architects seem so uninterested in offering some kind of alternative, speculative space to that of speculative capital.

'with the destruction of the '60s, at least they had the excuse that they were building the New Jerusalem'

What, then, of the promised 'agitation', or of positive proposals? OPEN Dalston is clearly one such example, holding out the possibility that an area can at least attempt to resist gentrification. Elsewhere the proposals range from small-scale improvements in the urban experience to some fairly empty-headed art practices. In the former category there is Heather Ring's proposal for a 'guerilla greenbelt', bringing together the *ad hoc* plantings on the disused edges of urban space. It's a proposal which will no doubt make the city look marginally nicer until the building contractors tear out the *lobelia*. But, pitched against the combined arsenal of the developers, the banks and their pliant councils, it seems more an act of mourning than of resistance, although at least Ring's proposal to unify these scattered plantings has some totalising ambition. In the other category, we have Hilary Powell's piece on the 2012 Olympics, a whimsically *retardataire* lament on the lack of good old British Blitz Spirit in the Olympics, its lamentable gigantism. Why, she asks, can't it be just a bit nicer, a bit more like the 'austerity Olympics' of 1948, show more of 'the DIY

Image: Philip Powell & Hidalgo Moya's Churchill Gardens Estate, Plimlico, London, 1947-62

ethos of making do and getting by, keeping calm and carrying on'. The possibility of imagining large-scale interventions or communal spaces is still mostly bypassed in favour of preemptively ineffectual notions of micro-resistance. In *Critical Cities* this alternately entails picturesque images of Japanese tent cities, or, in one of several 'curated interviews' here, one contributor praising how Dubai's indentured workers use the ultra-motorised city in an unplanned manner, carving out their own spaces. Regardless, a slave who 'creatively' 'subverts' space is still a slave.

While *Critical Cities* shows certain academics, planners, architects and artists inching towards some kind of break with urbanist orthodoxy, it's still too tied into it to truly convince. This makes it all the more remarkable that *Ground Control*, written by a former *Financial Times* staffer as a distillation of a series of reports for think-tanks, is so ferocious, so precise and so instructive in its comprehensive critique of British neoliberal urban policy. However, when it comes to alternatives Minton falters too, albeit with rather less bathos than some of the authors in *Critical Cities*. The scope does not entail the latter's trips to various Global Cities, there are no rhetorical

Image: Exchange Square in Manchester

excursions to Shenzen, Dubai or Tokyo, while Manchester and Liverpool get as much attention as East London. The specific focus on the British city makes it a case study in a particularly extreme variant of neoliberalism, which untangles the acronyms, catchphrase policies and quangos that administer its urban policy rather than adding another layer of jargon. Although Minton is no theorist and certainly no Marxist, this book is an excellent example of the kind of critical, materialist geography which could – and should – replace the tired focus on micro-subversions and micro-resistances.

Ground Control begins with an analysis of Canary Wharf, which Minton sees as the first draft of a new urbanism that has spread from there across Britain. She stresses that Blairite policy here is a peculiar outgrowth of both post-war *dirigisme* and Thatcherism, in the form of the ubiquitous Urban Development Corporations. Set up on the model of the New Town Development Corporations of the Attlee era, which had enormous and fundamentally unaccountable power over land, planning and building, areas of London, Tyneside and Liverpool essentially became exempt from democratic control in the 1980s, lest regeneration be compromised by 'loony left' Labour councils. Before selling up to developers, these instruments of state would create privately owned, privately patrolled enclaves at enormous public expense. These were expanded under New Labour into a dizzying amount of quangos and acronyms, but the major case study in the book is Manchester – and not the least of *Ground Control*'s grim pleasures is Minton's striking redress to the Mancunian boosterism of the last two decades. Rather than taking control of a small area, she notes that the entire centre of Manchester is run as a 'Business Improvement District', specifically by the private company Cityco, creating what she calls a 'pseudo-private space – streets and open spaces which are publicly owned but are actually privately controlled'. Minton argues persuasively that the reasoning behind this is linked closely with Blairism's 'respect agenda' (particularly in the form of the Anti-Social Behaviour Order), to a concern with security and public order, the fear of the mob. So in the case of Greater Manchester there is a situation where, in Salford, more is spent on the issuing of ASBOs than on youth services, and where the 'transformed' centre and docks barricade themselves against an outskirts of criminalised poverty.

Another of *Ground Control*'s great strengths is its stress on the interdependence of government and business, with massive state programmes aimed essentially at creating a more lucrative market. The most impressive of these, which she profiles in alarming detail, is the 'Pathfinder' Housing Market Renewal Scheme. In essence, this was an attempt to create in northern post-industrial cities a housing boom to balance London's, through the demolition of huge swathes of terraces, council houses and flats, using the same apparatus of compulsory purchase and clearance that was used in the post-war decades, although this time employed to very different ends – to increase demand for housing, rather than to rehouse the population in more sanitary, if perhaps less picturesque circumstances. She quotes one Liverpudlian campaigner: 'with the destruction of the sixties, at least they had the excuse that they were building the New Jerusalem. Now it's all about land deals'. The book makes clear that there was and is extensive opposition to Pathfinder, but that legal victories or upheld complaints came up against a rigged system – while 'the independent evaluation of the programme commissioned by the government was undertaken by Nevin Leather Associates, a consultancy co-founded by Brendan Nevin – the architect of Pathfinder himself.' One of the many upshots of this alliance between state and capital is a lucrative market for unregulated private landlords.

In theoretical terms, *Ground Control* sets up an opposition between two pillars of recent planning orthodoxy: Oscar Newman, author of the influential *Defensible Space*, whose paranoid, militaristic approach to urban design has been important in local councils ever since it was picked up by Essex County Council in the 1970s, and Jane Jacobs, proto-gentrifier in 1960s Greenwich Village and author of *The Death and Life of Great American Cities*. The two are often conflated as critics of Modernist planning and design, the zoned spaces of spaced-out towers and open space without 'streets'. Minton argues that they are in fact very different thinkers. While Newman helped create the delusion that crime could be 'designed out', that design itself could create social peace by excluding strangers and creating spaces which are tightly controlled (by residents or otherwise), Jacobs' idea of 'eyes on the street' is seen as a more organic, less relentlessly paranoid approach to a similar problem, where the built paraphernalia of security is less important than ensuring street life. As a critique of Modernist planning, it's decidedly less shallow than that of *Critical Cities*, although the 1960s remain a swear word. Whether this opposition works or not, it's clear that 'defensible space' remains enormously influential on urban design policies, whether in the gated communities of the affluent or the subtler enclosure of the remnants of social housing. One of the many alarming creatures in *Ground Control*'s Blairite bestiary is Secured By Design, a series of police checks which must be passed by any new development. She introduces this by discussing a housing association project which Hans Van der Heijden of BIQ Architecten worked on in Liverpool. They planned an open, 'continental' development, and were told in no uncertain terms that, according to the Secured By Design rules, the development must 'be surrounded by walls with sharp steel pins or broken glass on top of them, CCTV, and only one gate into the estate'. Despite having the support of residents, BIQ were sacked from the project and something containing the above was built in its place.

When it comes to suggestions for ways to redress this grim situation, much of what Minton has to offer is sensible enough (although beyond our undead neo-liberal political parties) – an end to obsessive security, more council housing, more housing co-operatives and more local democracy. Unfortunately, the urban renaissance still has some hold over *Ground Control*, most notably in the uncritical praise for the supposedly fairer policies of Switzerland, Italy, Denmark or the Netherlands. Yet while the cities of these countries may have more open public spaces and better housing design, they seem far more affected than urban Britain by a very particular kind of fear – of non-European intruders – and all have a more powerful far-right than the UK. Minton misses how the UK can be less segregated than continental Europe, especially in the capital and the larger cities. Similarly, she has some incongruous praise for the re-use of space by artists or 'creative' property developers, which in Manchester and East London especially was always a handmaiden to gentrification. As Sukhdev Sandhu points out in one of *Critical Cities*' few genuinely 'critical' contributions, this process is well established, and in places like Brick Lane serves to increase segregation and mutual distrust rather than lessen it. As a work of critique (and interdisciplinary research) *Ground Control* is immeasurably superior to *Critical Cities*. It's interesting, given how Ricky Burdett, in *Critical Cities*, talks of 'poking at the establishment but wanting to engage with it', that it takes a relatively establishment figure – a sociologist and journalist rather than an aesthete or academic – to offer a convincing attack on the urban delusions of the last 15 years.

Info:

Deepa Naik & Trenton Oldfield, eds., *Critical Cities – Ideas, Knowledge and Agitation from Emerging Urbanists*, London: Myrtle Court Press, 2009.

Anna Minton, *Ground Control – Fear and Happiness in the 21st Century City*, London: Penguin, 2009.

This Is Not a Gateway: http://www.thisisnotagateway.net

Owen Hatherley <owenhatherley@googlemail.com> is a freelance writer on political aesthetics for, among others, *Building Design*, the *Guardian* and the *New Statesman*, and a researcher at Birkbeck College, London. He is the author of *Militant Modernism* (Zero Books, 2009)

Image: Mattin and Taku Unami, *Distributing Vulnerability to the Affective Classes*, performance at the Rigoletto, Paris, 14 December 2009

AGAINST REPRESENTATION: A REVOLUTION IN FRONT OF YOU

By taking everything as possible material for improvisation (not just sounds, but ideas, affects, power relations, hidden structures contained within the room...) it is possible to develop a practice of 'extreme site-specificity'. Noise artist Mattin probes the enigma of radical performativity

The representation of the working class radically opposes itself to the working class.
– Guy Debord, 'Thesis 100', *Society of the Spectacle*

Representation as a Form of Mediation: Fragmentation/Separation

Representation in politics can be seen as a form of delegation. One ceases to take responsibility for certain acts and thoughts, relegating it to somebody else who will speak for you. In representative democracy an ordinary person does not have the possibility of developing the specific language needed to speak to power or authority. A separation is created between everyday life and the moments when political decisions are made in society or the community. As Guy Debord pointed out, 'representation separates life from experience', similar to the separation of disciplines, the division of labour, and the distinction between work and leisure. However, as Jean-Luc Guionnet remarked to me, Debord criticised representation without criticising the language that he himself was using. As representation is the typical medium of artistic practice, it is no wonder Debord and other Situationists wanted to supersede art. They desired life without separation.

As long as we accept art as a separate discipline it will be more difficult to produce concrete and direct political change through artistic practice. Similarly, to think that political action can only happen in the realm of politics or in the streets would also be a way of accepting that separation.

Never before have we had so much access to self-representation, nor has our subjectivity been such a product of representation

Some questions emerged during a discussion: who is the political subject today? Where is the political struggle today? Surely many years have passed since the concise criticism of the spectacle by Debord. Capitalism has continued to develop powerful and complex forms of alienation, the most recent of which surely include forms of biopower and social networking. People are no longer simply spectators of their own lives through representation, as Debord argued, but create their reality through the representations available on MySpace and Facebook. Profit flows from people's sharing of creativity, emotions and intimate information – all of which is surely very helpful for market researchers, and the police.

We're no longer contemplating our life through certain forms of representation. We've internalised the spectacle to such an extent that the way we relate to each other, our interactivity in everyday life and experience, is reproducing it, not with a feeling of passivity or distance, but with an intense desire to enjoy ourselves, be ourselves and be connected. Have your say, produce, write, listen, start your own blog, comment in online forums, express yourself. Never before have we had so much access to self-representation, and never before has our subjectivity been such a product of representation.

All is not that bad on the internet. New realities and ways of working together are being built thanks to the Free Software movement, a very interesting example of how to counter the division between the realms of production and consumption. But for the spectacle, consuming is also no longer enough; being connected is now required. Could this be a more intimate form of separation? What about all those iPhoners who are half here, half there? Separation before being connected, separation from oneself?

Now let's imagine we are in the same room with Gregg Bordowitz. At his talk at the Whitney Independent Study Program, we were impressed by his attentiveness to what was happening in the room. What type of relations were being built there and then? What type of environments were being created? He managed to create a different type of atmosphere in the space where so many discussions had already taken place. He created perplexity, and he inspired us, making us aware of the politics in the room and certain repressive relations taking place there. Sometimes a revolution is needed in the room.

How much are you willing to engage the situation that you are in?

The possibilities of a revolutionary practice are already in front of us. It is a matter of penetrating the surface of our reality which appears to be so neutral and free of interest. At the same time, we can feel a spectral hand making us behave in a certain way. The hand of the normalisation process that does not let things get disrupted. The means to disturb this neutrality might be extremely simple; from talking to making noise, from acting different than usual to being utterly honest, from saying the most intimate things in public to being totally quiet when you should be having fun. To stop being so self-conscious about your reputation could also help. Surely it would mean to give up at least momentarily the restrictions of being the 'yourself' of MySpace and Facebook. Why not become someone else? Fuck knows who, perhaps The Stranger.

Improvisation: Elusive and Unstable

Sabotage all representation!

– The Invisible Committee, *The Coming Insurrection*

In speaking of improvisation we not only discuss the production of particular sounds or events but the production of social spaces as well. We invoke this as both a strategic term and a conceptual tool. Improvisation can therefore refer both to experimental music making as well as everyday and mundane practices. Improvisation as having a long historical use outside the realm of contemporaty art, cannot be identified with an origin nor as a term coined by a group of artists or musicians (as oppossed to Conceptual Art, Institutional Critique, EAI...). Obviously anybody can do it without having to understanding the complex issues related to a specific discourse. Improvisation as opposed to other kinds of music making or practices, has no fidelity to any roots or origins. It is by default heretic. Where applied, improvisation brings about glimpses of instability. If it is working, its elusive qualities evade solidification and commodification – at least in the moment.

Towards a Dense Atmosphere: Radical Performativity and Site-Specificity

Within the context of art, is it possible to have a non-representational relationship to reality? If yes, this is surely done by acknowledging all the specificities of the room. One should try to activate the room as much as possible and disrupt previous habits and behaviours to create different ones. In other words, to go against the normalisation process. I have found improvisation to be a practice which takes into account everything happening in the room. Not to create something new that later could be used elsewhere, but as a way of intensifying the moment through changing social relations.

Improvisation can be an extreme form of site-specificity as well as a radical, intimate and immanent self-criticality. As there is no need to defend or build a position for future situations, improvisation always points towards self-destruction.

We could see improvisation as pure mediality with no outside to itself, as pure means without end, countering any form of separation, fragmentation or individuality. When can one feel this activation of the space taking effect? When there is a dense atmosphere which makes you aware that something important is at stake. As there are no predetermined categories or words to describe this experience, what is at stake is very difficult to articulate. Because of the difficulties of assimilating it or immediately understanding it, this affective strangeness counters the normalisation process. When this dense atmosphere is produced, the people involved become painfully aware of their social position and usual behaviour. If the density of the atmosphere is sufficient it can become physical, disturbing our senses and producing strange feelings in our bodies. Through such a multi-sensorial disruption in the appearance of neutrality, one gets the sense of being in a strange place – not really knowing where to stand. We become vulnerable. Every movement or word becomes significant. Once you are there, there is no way back. What is created is not a unified sense of space or time, but a hererotopia where one location contains different spaces and temporalities. Previous hierarchies and established organisations of space are exposed. The traditional time of the performance and distribution of attention (the audience's respectful behaviour towards the performers etc.) are left behind. If one goes far enough, actively distributing one's vulnerability, these hierarchies could be diffused, not to give a false sense of equality, but to produce alternative social relations of time and space. The creation of an affective class?

Don't get me wrong, I am not talking about 'relational aesthetics' where some audience interactivity adds cultural capital to some bland art works done by very concrete artists with dubious ideologies.

Estrangement

Brecht's *Verfremundungseffekt* (poorly translated as 'estrangement effect') tries to get rid of the fourth wall in the theatre by distancing and disrupting the illusion separating the audience from the stage/performer, making evident their 'passive' and 'alienated' condition. This in turn makes them understand how constructed the situation is.

In improvisation the estrangement effect is doubled, as the condition of the actor or performer is also disrupted. As both the performers and the audience find themselves in a condition that they could not have anticipated before, the separation between them is no longer so clear.

Right now, in whatever situation you are in, how much are you willing to give up?

A dense atmosphere in improvisation reveals the conservative construction of the situation (audience, performance, manager, curator). It produces the desire for a new set of conditions. There are no prescriptions for improvisation. The goal is to create an unprecedented situation – strange for everybody, without a didactic or presupposed agenda. In his text 'The Emancipated Spectator', Jacques Rancière uses the example of Joseph Jacotot, a French professor in the 19th century who tried to teach his students what he himself did not know. In doing so, he took as his starting point the equality of intelligence, negating claims to mastery of knowledge. In Rancière's

How much are you willing to engage the situation that you are in?

words, Jacotot was 'calling for intellectual emancipation against the standard idea of the instruction of the people'. Performing the authority of knowledge (like Debord's criticism or Brecht's didactics) reproduces the logic of mastery, even when its deconstruction is intended. Brecht plays certain strategies against each other (i.e. introducing social realism into an epic or romantic scenario) in order for their techniques and effects to become evident.

Saying intimate things in public or being quiet when you should be having fun disturb neutrality

However his didactics continually distance the viewer from what they do not know, from what they still 'have to learn'. Rancière advocates thinking differently about seeing and hearing – not as acts of passivity but as 'ways of interpreting the world', as ways of transforming and reconfiguring it. He is against this pedagogical distance as well as any idea of genre or discipline, but he doesn't go far enough in explaining how this oppositionality could be enacted. Rejection of these inequalities is not enough. We need an alternative way to experience life which is indifferent to hierarchical knowledge claims. Again, interpretation would require mediation, as one would be reflecting on the situation, rather than *being* in the situation.

The question is how to be 'in' the situation as much as possible, with minimum reflection in order to explore, live and experience the precise moment. Here I am not aligned with Feuerbach's romantic idea of truth as unseparateness, but claim that the Real itself does not contain these separations. These separations can be understood as ideologically and historically constructed truths which are used to mediate our experience of the Real. However, the closer we get to the Real, the less these ready-made truths help us to live it or experience it. If we are 'in' enough, we might be able to leave behind our previous preconceptions, prescriptions, and ideologies.

'Real' here is to be understood quite straightforwardly, as what happens 'for real' simply because it's happening here and now. It's connected to the sense in which one can have a real pain, and behave as though that pain were real: indeed, this is an interesting characteristic of children's playing, when they encounter pain, they expressed it. This is not to say that 'real' in its everyday adjectival sense doesn't harbour a powerful but complicated connection with the Real as noun, whether François Laruelle's or Jacques Lacan's.

Only the production of new and radical concepts in a language indifferent to the dominant structures would help us to understand the particularities of the situation in the dense atmosphere that we have created.

The Stranger

> *The Stranger or the identity of the real is non-reflected, lived, experienced, consumed while remaining in itself without the need to alienate itself through representation.*
>
> – François Laruelle

To what extent would you detourn yourself in the situation you are in?

When improvisation is successful, it puts everybody in an strange situation; it makes us strangers. In his non-Marxism, François Laruelle uses the concept of The Stranger to describe a more radical and universal concept of the proletariat. The Stranger is a radically immanent and performative, non-representational, non-normative thinking subject. It is a force (of) thought and a heretic in the sense of refusing authority and tradition. As Ray Brassier puts it:

> The Stranger: is the name for the Subject of practice-of-theory, modelled ('cloned') on given material (philosophical, but in this instance sonic/music/aesthetic/cultural

> etc.), but determined by [the?] real of the last instance (=One etc.), whose immanence it effectuates. The Stranger-subject is what you become when you think-practice-perform in radical immanence.

For the sake of space let me butcher Laruelle's complex system of non-philosophy. Laruelle is trying to explore the Real through radical immanence without adding layers of either reflection or representation, through which we otherwise mediate our experiences. In order to understand the concept of The Stranger we have to understand 'Determination-in-the-Last-Instance' (DLI). Originally the term was invented by Marx-Engels for historical materialism, and developed by Althusser for his analysis of infrastructure/superstructure (which in the last instance remains reciprocally co-constituted by what it determines). For Laruelle, the DLI is simultaneously real, universal, immanent, heterogeneous, and irreversible.

If the density of the atmosphere is sufficient it can become physical, disturbing our senses

The DLI is not simply an immanent causality but radical immanence itself. A syntax without synthesis which excludes reciprocity, convertibility, systematicity, finality, formalism, materialism and technologism. Laruelle is not trying to empirically prove his concepts but instead use them as self-evident thoughts which correlate to the Real. The DLI does not escape from itself or alienate itself. The DLI is the causality of unforeseeable (non-definable and non-demonstrable) theoretical and pragmatic emergence – if we look at the etymology of improvisation we find that its Latin root 'improvisus' means 'unforeseen'. It is practice-of-theory which is an event in itself. The DLI invalidates or suspends theoretical authority and any claims to knowledge of the Real. The Real cannot correspond to a doctrine or a discipline, however it can be 'cloned' into a concept and from there you try to deal with the immanence of the concept itself, taking it as an axiom rather than using it to understand or determine the Real. You cannot get yourself into the Real, but you can clone it into a concept, and then remain as close as possible by dealing performatively with the concept, with the minimum reflection possible.

Following Laruelle we can take improvisation as an axiom, in the sense that one cannot really define when one is or is not improvising (since so many questions arise around individual free will, subjectivity, and ideology; questions which I don't think can ever be satisfactorily resolved). By adopting this axiomatic approach to improvisation as a domain to which one can bring ideas, decisions, and concepts as ways of narrowing down or focusing where the improvisation is going to happen, one can look closely into a specific area. Everything can be a tool for improvisation and we can learn a lot from feminist thinkers such as Judith Butler and Peggy Phelan about how to bring the notion of performativity down from its conceptual use (such as in Laruelle's) in order to intensify an encounter with the concept that the 'personal is political'.

Radical concepts can enable a radical critique from within, without respect to the master terms such as capital and heteronormalism.

J.K. Gibson-Graham says in *The End of Capitalism (As We Knew It): A Feminist Critique of Political Economy*,

> Capitalism is the phallus or 'master term' within a system of social differentiation. Capitalist industrialization grounds the distinction between core (the developed world) and periphery (the so-called Third World).

If we understand capitalism as the 'master term', then the 'Stranger-in-the-last-instance' is the most particular and vulnerable subject and it cannot be represented by either the dominant hegemonic order or the working class. The Stranger is too particular and site-specific to be subsumed by other universalised concepts. The Stranger is the ultimate impossible subject and only respects the authority of the Lived and Experienced rather than the Represented.

Thanks to Lisa Rosendhal, David Baumflek, Jean-Luc Guionnet, Ray Brassier, Seiji Murayama, Emma Hedditch, Ilya Lipkin, Jennifer Kennedy, Anthony Iles, Josephine Berry Slater, Howard Slater & Henry Flynt

Mattin <mattin@mattin.org> is a Basque artist working mostly with noise and improvisation. His work seeks to address the social and economic structures of experimental music production through live performance, recordings and writing, http://www.mattin.org

Image: Vestas and Lego display at Copenhagen Airport

HOPENHAGEN AGAINST HOPE

Amidst the general eco-panic and its commodification, Ilya Lipkin travelled to the Copenhagen Summit to witness capitalism's first last chance at preserving a climate conducive to its growth

Situating COP15: Capitalist Logic and Subjectivity

In attempting to process COP15, the UN Summit on Global Warming that took place in Copenhagen this past December 2009, what must be avoided is a 'neutral' and static representation of the highly politicised dynamics, both global and local, that constituted this event. Writing these lines, I immediately recognise the uneasy tension between providing information that more or less accurately historicises and recounts the summit, and the need to avoid rendering objective or continuous that which is not. This desire for subjective discontinuity stems from the urgent necessity to reject all depictions of the global warming crisis as anything other than a political problem. Without a concrete grounding in the political, any attempt to address the economic dimension of climate change would end in abstraction. Thus, when I say 'subjective discontinuity' I do not here mean a kind of relativism in relation to experience. I speak of the discontinuity of the real, and the understanding that to become a subject is fundamentally tied up with the collective imagining and militant commitment to that which is deemed impossible in the present order of things.[1] I believe that any understanding of COP15 must begin with the assertion of one's subjectivity in the face of 'common sense'. This insistence helps in turn reveal what is at stake in our reflecting on COP15: much as with other recent events tied to deep structural dynamics (such as the financial crisis), our interpretation and understanding of this event directly informs the horizon of political possibilities available to us in the present.

Capitalism tends to suppress such a conception of the subject by routinely and vigorously foreclosing possible alternatives to the way in which social relations are currently structured. In the face of every crisis tied to the unsustainability of a continuous growth economy, attempts at envisioning an emancipatory politics in the present are routinely equated with a return to totalitarian fantasies. For example, while hardly radical and clearly problematic in their own right, efforts to move towards the socialisation of healthcare or the drafting of legislation to regulate financial markets were both immediately denounced throughout much of the American media as a conspiracy by the left to slowly pave the way to communism. These reactive, at times delusional claims are generally coupled with a slew of essentialist notions and a return to an Enlightenment era humanism filtered through current modes of representational politics (primarily through the equation of 'inalienable freedoms for all' with free markets and the right to private property). This should come as no surprise: since the rise of neoliberalism in the late '70s and certainly since the collapse of the Soviet Union, we have been living in a period of restoration. However, it is important to keep in mind that the suppression of alternative visions of social relations is not only connected to a project of the restoration and maintenance of class power. It is also fundamental to the continuous and uninterrupted process of territorialisation, most obviously in the ceaseless and violent hammering out of new zones of investment for surplus capital. The current ideological dominance of the leitmotifs of 'freedom' and 'human rights' plays a central role in maintaining the imperative of continuous growth, which in turn guarantees that the capitalist system lives to see another day. Has it not been drilled into us, since the times of Reagan and Thatcher, that 'there is no alternative?'

we should reject all depictions of the global warming crisis as anything other than a political problem

With this in mind, it is difficult to see the COP15 summit as anything other than the extension of this very process of territorialisation and recuperation to the genuine problem of climate change. The primary function of the summit was to carve out new zones of investment and technical development. It is capital's indifference to the qualitative configuration of things – so long as they can be brought into alignment with market forces – that explains its extraordinary ability to accommodate the most diverse demands, including environmentalist ones. While paying lip service to the global warming crisis, the political leaders gathered at COP15 were never genuinely interested in exploring the fundamental relation between continuous growth, the depletion of natural resources and the destruction of the environment. A glance at the Copenhagen Accord, drafted up behind closed doors by the US, China, Brazil, India and South Africa, and recognised by the Parties to the UN Framework Convention on Climate Change, reveals the summit's true objective: 'to use markets, to increase the cost-effectiveness of, and to promote, mitigation actions [against global warming].'[2]

The Copenhagen Accord, one of the few measurable 'accomplishments' of the summit, goes on to say that

> the collective commitment by developed countries is to provide new and additional resources [...] investments through international institutions, approaching USD 30 billion for the period of 2010-12 [...] with a goal of mobilizing USD 100 billion a year by 2020.[3]

The funding for this type of investment will come from 'a wide variety of sources, public and private, bilateral and multilateral, including alternative sources of finance.'[4] To determine how this funding will be distributed and put to work, all of the investment capital will flow through the newly established Copenhagen Green Climate Fund. But the grisly record of another famous international fund, the IMF, makes it clear that even 'public' investment of this nature expects a return, and hence 'structural adjustment' policies that wreak wave upon wave of social dislocation.[5]

What is therefore strongly implied in the Copenhagen Accord is that relief from the ill effects of global warming and access to the technologies and capital that would allow developing nations to convert to sustainable modes of production comes at a price. Namely, a series of structural changes in compliance with the guidelines of those providing the resources. This should come as no surprise, as much of the thinking behind COP15 finds its origins in the neoliberal transition from the social-welfare model of the state, that took place in the '70s throughout much of Western Europe and America. However, the process of deindustrialisation and financialisation in the West heralded by this transition – a process that led to the current global hegemonic configuration – is currently in crisis. As the historian Giovanni Arrighi has pointed out, a period of financial expansion always occurs when the material expansion of productive forces reaches a limit. Financial expansion too has its limits: Arrighi refers to this as the 'autumn' of a particular hegemon.[6] In other words, financial expansion is the concluding phase of a particular process of leadership in accumulation, resulting in eventual displacement by another leader. Or, as Karl Marx put it: autumn becomes a spring elsewhere, producing a sequence of interconnected developments.

Judging by the most recent market collapse, it would be fair to hypothesise that the process of financial expansion in the West has slowed down markedly, with the consequence that the configuration of global power is likely itself in deep and rapid transition. The COP15 summit reveals exactly how, on a global scale, political leaders from the dominant nations have attempted to capitalise on the problem of global warming to serve their own interests: as yet another tool for the maintenance of the current order of power and wealth, as well as a potential zone to be cultivated for the restoration of markets and the creation of new investment opportunities.

The pitfall in this type of thinking is the perfectly circular logic it requires. The leaders gathered at COP15 adopted neoliberal strategies to think through a problem that essentially stems from the type of growth demanded by capitalism.

Image: Protesters liberate one tonne of CO2

The summit's anxious reluctance to think of global warming as a political problem that is inextricable from the structure of social relations is yet another symptom of the tautological self-coherence of the ideologies of capital. If we believe that there is no alternative, then no alternative will present itself – no matter how devastating the human and environmental consequences. Hence, again, the urgency of refusing this purported 'logic' and of centring the debate on its very terms.

Spectacle and Local Politics – COP15 and the City of Copenhagen

Equally as disturbing as the way in which COP15 was instrumentalised on a global scale, however, is the way this summit was put to work locally by the city of Copenhagen – or, as it was dubbed for the duration of the summit, 'Hopenhagen'. This play on words, in all of its spectacular buffoonery, was very much in line with the general grooming of the city during COP15. I became aware of it immediately upon my arrival at Kastrup airport, as I was greeted by an artistic collaboration between Vestas and Lego in the form of several large windmills made of a million plastic blocks. Children and adults alike stopped to stare and photograph themselves in front of these creations and the miniature cities beneath. Upon leaving the airport and walking through the streets of the city, I encountered various posters, signs and advertisements promoting 'green' products, 'green' events, 'green' concerts… . A particularly haunting recurrent image featured various individuals, probably meant to look like 'third world natives,' staring back at me and inquiring: 'What future do you want to live in?'

COP15 played a central role in the cleansing, gentrification and branding of the eco-friendly utopia of 'Hopenhagen'

This fusion of consumerism, spectacularised culture and a sense of feel-good optimism reached its surreal peak during the speeches leading up to the main demonstration on 12 December. The over 100,000 people gathered in front of the parliament building found themselves addressed by the Danish actor Thure Lindhardt, who devoted a lengthy portion of his speech to exhorting the demonstrators to remain peaceful. Next up was the fashion model Helena Christensen – absurdist theatre at its best. Reading haltingly from a prepared statement, Ms. Christensen spoke of her concern about global warming, assured us of her activism, and encouraged us all to attend her exhibition of photographs at a local gallery. The theme of her show: the effects of global warming in Peru.

special prisons were built in an old Carlsberg warehouse: 37 twelve square meter cages, each designed to hold ten protesters

All of these campaigns and speeches served a single purpose: the promotion of Denmark as a progressive and prosperous nation that is sensitive to the eco-troubles of the world. COP15 played a central role in the larger project of cleansing, gentrification, and branding of the eco-friendly and global utopia of 'Hopenhagen'. Behind this depiction, of course, lies a 'common-sensical' understanding of real estate as investment and a desire to cultivate a business-friendly climate. One could not help but get the feeling that the parties responsible for these campaigns were fully aware of their strategic function in the larger ongoing local fight against the various activist and community groups resisting the forces of gentrification. Of course, the more pervasive and obvious these self-congratulatory promotional tactics, the greater the sense of disconnect: the corporate image of Copenhagen that was produced for and through the summit was utterly at odds with the daily stream of news of police violence and arrests, general confusion, and repeated breakdowns in the official talks among international delegates at the Bella Center.

In reality, squarely underpinning the sunny rhetoric was a series of calculated decisions by the Danish parliament that included the implementation of new laws facilitating preventive arrests and cracking down on civil disobedience during the summit. This 'protest package' gave police the right to detain civilians for up to 12 hours even when no law had been infringed.[7]

'Disturbing the peace' or disobeying police orders during a protest would result in a 40-day imprisonment.[8] Furthermore, special prisons were built in an old Carlsberg warehouse: 37 twelve square metre cages, each designed to hold ten protesters.[9] Arbitrary harassment and detainment were effectively legalised, and the contradiction between the official progressive rhetoric and the reality of a police state made absolutely blatant.

Even more worrying, though by no means shocking, was the fact that while these laws were purportedly passed to prevent disturbances during a visit by global leaders, they will remain on the books. The consequences for future demonstrations, protests and actions are drastic and potentially devastating. In a city endowed with a strong anti-capitalist activist movement, resistance to state power will, from now on, be more difficult still.

A Demonstration – Collective Resistance to COP15

The panoply of forces of resistance, global and local, in all of their multiplicity, contradiction and collective power, was in full evidence during the main demonstration against COP15 on 12 December, 2009. Following the aforementioned speeches on the steps of the Danish parliament, a gigantic assortment of bodies, banners and vehicles, with the usual police accompaniment, set into motion on a long, slow march towards the Bella Center. My friends and I began our trek alongside a truck to the sounds of Max Romeo and the Upsetters' 'I Chase the Devil.' As the hours wore on, our collective mood was stoked by a rousing speech made by Lars Grenaa of the Communist Workers' Party. Speaking in English, Mr. Grenaa powerfully and succinctly outlined the relationship between COP15, the interests of capital and the need for system change if the problem of global warming is to be addressed properly. While he delivered his message, a large banner reading 'FCK FCK FCK the System' elicited smiles and cheers as it swayed from the back of his truck.

High spirits and a sense of excitement pervaded the march, even as the mass of protesters ebbed and flowed. At one point, rumours began to circulate of people being held back. We would not find out until much later in the night that, indeed, one thousand demonstrators had been preemptively arrested and made to sit hand-cuffed on the cold ground for several long hours.[10] Many soiled their pants because they were not allowed access to a bathroom. These arrests occurred under the transparent pretext that those detained were plotting a violent action and were not part of the 'official demonstration'. However, because of a lack of communication and the massive police presence forcing the protesters forward, we continued on our way blissfully unaware of what had just transpired.

Sunset came and went, and in the glow of the street lights an atmosphere of celebration descended upon us. The music from the trucks got louder and more upbeat, people began dancing furiously in a throbbing ocean of banners, signs, balloons and flags. Many who lived on the streets we marched down threw open their windows, hung out banners and waved their support to the demonstrators. For a fleeting moment it felt as though our differences had been genuinely superseded by collective euphoria: no more 'you', no more 'me' – we were one organic mass that cried out 'NO!' to COP15 and 'NO!' to capitalism.

By the time we arrived at the Bella Center, however, much of this powerful energy had dissipated; a feeling of deep ambivalence hung over the conclusion of this protest. Perhaps this was unavoidable: after all, this demonstration had been organised largely by NGOs, it obeyed the guidelines set forth by the Danish authorities, and those involved stopped short of engaging in a confrontation with the law. Admittedly, it would be presumptuous of me to speculate on exactly what drew protesters to this demonstration in the first place. This is especially true when 'protestors' refers not to a homogenous mass, but to a multiplicity of bodies with a wide range of backgrounds, political views and desires. After all, this demonstration brought together groups as varied as anarchist collectives, black-blocers, Greenpeace, Philippine fishermen, communists, social democrats, and a plethora of eco-activists. Yet it is clear that whatever the demands of each group or individual may have been, these demands were largely overdetermined by the circumstances through which they were made public. Cynicism aside, it is tempting to read the demonstration as a mass process of repressive desublimation: without confrontation, without transgression, without any rupturing of the rules set forth by power, it might easily seem that the protest functioned primarily as a collective emotional outlet. Such an experience has of course value in its own right, providing one

the protests were without confrontation, without transgression, a mass process of repressive desublimation

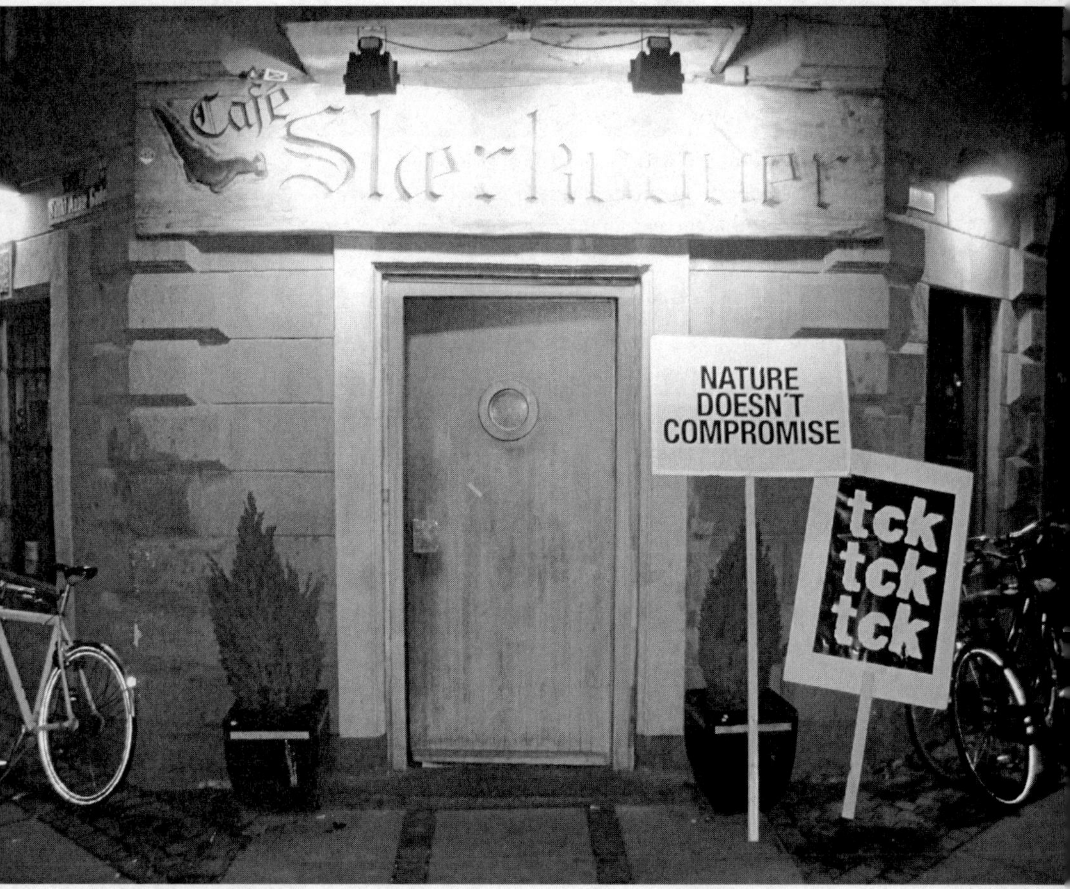

Image: 'My friends and I stood up, and slowly made our way to the nearest bar.'

with a momentary space in which to experience collectivity and to voice frustration. Ultimately, however, the political impact of this event was limited by its existence solely within a temporal and physical space granted to it by the authorities. As such, the demonstration could do little more than legitimate the power of the state and underscore its 'tolerance' towards dissent.

It was not long after this demonstration, on Monday the 14th to be precise, that the Danish authorities cleared up any lingering illusion concerning the power dynamics between demonstrators and the police within the city. Late that evening, approximately three hundred people were arrested as the police stormed Christiania with tear gas, following a talk given by Michael Hardt and Naomi Klein.[11] Many had to find refuge in the free city itself for the duration of the night, as leaving without harassment or arrest was next to impossible. Furthermore, the action planned at the talk – entering the Bella Center and encouraging the delegates to come out and speak to the activists – was also brutally foiled on Wednesday the

16th.[12] As the summit drew to a close, the activists and demonstrators gathered in Copenhagen were faced with the harsh reality that, at least this time around, victory would remain elusive.

Postscript

On one of the last nights of the summit, I happened to walk with friends past the Folkets Hus in Nørrebro. On an adjacent street, someone had just set fire to a dumpster and as black smoke filled the air, eager youths ran up to feed it wood and detritus. I immediately thought of somehow incorporating this fire into my text; it invited meaning. As we were all exhausted from the events of the week, we sat down on some stones nearby and watched the flames tickle the night sky. The smell of burning plastic wafted through the air. I tried to jot down a few notes, to no avail. After some time, I began to suspect that what drew me to this image was that it made no demands: it was simply, stupidly there. Days later, I thought again about how to politicise it, how to recuperate it, speak to it and of it, but this encounter remained elusive: an act of wordless violence that had nothing to do with 'politics'. That night, when the police and the fire brigade arrived, my friends and I stood up, and slowly made our way to the nearest bar.

Footnotes

1 My understanding of subject formation here draws heavily from the philosopher Alain Badiou and his definition of the subject as it appears in his book *Ethics*: 'I call "subject" the bearer of a fidelity, the one who bears a process of truth. The subject in no way pre-exists the process. He is absolutely nonexistent in the situation "before" the event. We might say that the process of truth induces a subject... to be sure, the militant enters into the composition of this subject, but once again it exceeds him.' Badiou goes on to say that 'Events are irreducible singularities, the "beyond the law" of situations. Each faithful truth process is an entirely invented immanent break with the situation.' Thus, the process of entering into subjectivity implies a break with the individual and calls for the 'becoming immortal' of the subject through the collective. And simultaneously, it insists on a commitment to the impossible of a situation because of the necessity of an immanent break with all that provided the

Image: 1,000 demonstrators handcuffed in the cold

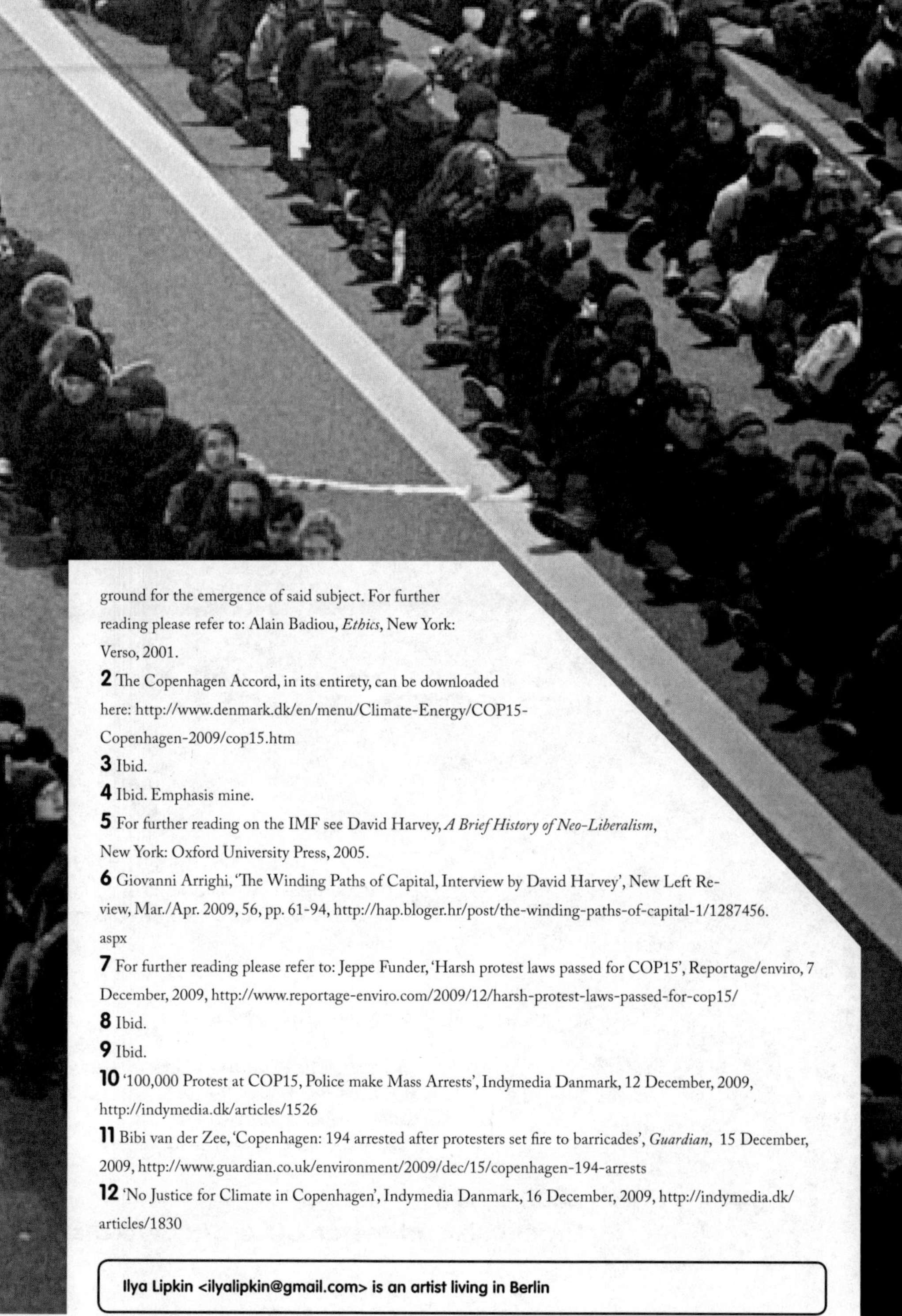

ground for the emergence of said subject. For further reading please refer to: Alain Badiou, *Ethics*, New York: Verso, 2001.

2 The Copenhagen Accord, in its entirety, can be downloaded here: http://www.denmark.dk/en/menu/Climate-Energy/COP15-Copenhagen-2009/cop15.htm

3 Ibid.

4 Ibid. Emphasis mine.

5 For further reading on the IMF see David Harvey, *A Brief History of Neo-Liberalism*, New York: Oxford University Press, 2005.

6 Giovanni Arrighi, 'The Winding Paths of Capital, Interview by David Harvey', New Left Review, Mar./Apr. 2009, 56, pp. 61-94, http://hap.bloger.hr/post/the-winding-paths-of-capital-1/1287456.aspx

7 For further reading please refer to: Jeppe Funder, 'Harsh protest laws passed for COP15', Reportage/enviro, 7 December, 2009, http://www.reportage-enviro.com/2009/12/harsh-protest-laws-passed-for-cop15/

8 Ibid.

9 Ibid.

10 '100,000 Protest at COP15, Police make Mass Arrests', Indymedia Danmark, 12 December, 2009, http://indymedia.dk/articles/1526

11 Bibi van der Zee, 'Copenhagen: 194 arrested after protesters set fire to barricades', *Guardian*, 15 December, 2009, http://www.guardian.co.uk/environment/2009/dec/15/copenhagen-194-arrests

12 'No Justice for Climate in Copenhagen', Indymedia Danmark, 16 December, 2009, http://indymedia.dk/articles/1830

Ilya Lipkin <ilyalipkin@gmail.com> is an artist living in Berlin

The Mute Archive - a special box set of Mute magazine back issues

Original copies of nearly every issue* of Mute from 1994 to the present - 42 issues, including special inserts, CDs, software and artworks

Mute has been publishing on culture, politics, and technology since 1994, earning an international reputation for originality, humour and intelligence. The first incarnation of *Mute* was a barely disguised replica of the Financial Times, printed on the same distinctive pink newsprint. Since then *Mute* evolved into a colour, highly graphic magazine, and finally into the hybrid print/web publication it is today.

Featuring many of the artists, writers and photographers who came to epitomise London's status as a creative hotbed, the Mute Archive is a great addition to an academic or personal library.

The Mute Archive includes:

The Broadsheet: Issues pilot - 7 (1994-1997)
The Glossies: Issues 8 – 24*
Coffee Table: Issues 25 – 29
POD: Volume II, issues 0-10

£200 + p&p
Order online at metamute.org/mutearchive

Institutional and credit card phone orders contact +44 (0)20 7377 6949
Skype mute.london or email lois@metamute.org for enquiries

*we regret that issue 9 is sold out

Magazine Subscription

MUTE

Get *Mute* delivered to your door for one year and guarantee to be first in line for our quarterly collection of provocative articles on culture, politics and technology

Subscription rates	individual		institutional/company	
	4 issues (1 year)	8 issues (2 years)	4 issues (1 year)	8 issues (2 years)
uk	☐ £20	☐ £38	☐ £35	☐ £67
europe	☐ £22	☐ £41	☐ £38	☐ £72
usa/ rest of world	☐ £25	☐ £46	☐ £43	☐ £82

Please tick the appropriate box.

I wish to pay by cheque/credit card.

☐ I enclose a cheque (GBP) made payable to Mute.

☐ Please charge my

☐ Visa ☐ Access ☐ Mastercard ☐ Switch

Card no.

Expiry date /

(Switch only) Issue number Start date /

Security code

Signature

name

address

town/city

post code

country

tel

email

INSTITUTIONAL OPTIONS:
W: metamute.org/subs
T: +44 (0)20 7377 6949
E: lois@metamute.org
A complete archive of *Mute* back issues is available

ADDRESS CHANGE:
If you are an existing subscriber needing to change your address, then please email us at lois@metamute.org

Subscribe online at metamute.org/subs or call our credit card hotline on +44 (0)20 7377 6949

Gift Subscriptions
If you are giving Mute to a friend, you can leave their details on completion of your purchase together with your own payment details.

Order online metamute.org/subs